Victories Without Violence

True stories of ordinary people coming through dangerous situations without using physical force.

Compiled by A. Ruth Fry

LIBERTY LITERARY WORKS
OCEAN TREE BOOKS
Santa Fe • 1986

Other books of related interest from Ocean Tree Books:

PEACE PILGRIM: Her Life and Work in Her Own Words
STEPS TOWARD INNER PEACE, also by Peace Pilgrim
PRAYERS OF THE WORLD: Familiar Prayers of Many Faiths
GANDHI'S SEVEN STEPS: A Way to Global Change

Please send for Ocean Tree's free catalog.

First American Edition.

Preface Copyright©1986 by Jennifer L. Goodwin.
Additional elements Copyright©1986 by Ocean Tree Books.

Rights to this work have been granted the publishers by Mrs. O. B. Taber and the estate of A. Ruth Fry. Printed in the United States of America.

This is a facsimile of the 1952 edition of Victories Without Violence, originally published in 1939 by Peace Book Club in England.

Co-published by:
  Liberty Literary Works
  1001 Atlantic Shores Blvd., #113
  Hallandale, Florida 33009
and
  Ocean Tree Books
  Post Office Box 1295
  Santa Fe, New Mexico 87504

ISBN: 0-943734-06-1
Library of Congress Catalog Card Number 85-43527

PREFACE TO THE AMERICAN EDITION

There was a little city with few men in it; and a great king came against and besieged it, building great siegeworks against it. But there was found in it a poor wise man, and he by his wisdom delivered the city. Yet no one remembered that poor man.

Ecclesiastes 9:14-15

W E LIVE by certain assumptions about human behavior that appear logical and self-evident. We assume, for example, that physical force "works", if we've got enough of it, for our own protection. So, many people buy guns for their homes, and we stockpile large numbers of weapons for national defense.

Yet statistics show that people with guns in their homes are far more likely to be injured or killed than those without them. And our billions of dollars of military hardware not only haven't made us feel secure, but in numerous confrontations (such as hostage situations) we have been helpless to protect our citizens abroad. Even when violence succeeds in the short term, it tends to have side effects and long term results that promote further conflict.

The true stories in this volume give evidence that there are patterns of human behavior, repeating over and over, that defy the conventional wisdom about the nature of power. They challenge our assumptions about the outcome of confrontations between persons of unequal strength — revealing that often the "stronger" does not prevail.

Though this book was first published many years ago, it is in no sense dated. Ruth Fry's Introduction is a concise gem that rings as true and wise today as the day it was written. Moreover, the reappearance of similar events during so many different times and places suggests that they may reveal universal truths. Ruth Fry revised the book and added new stories for more than a decade. In the course of over a year's recent research on the psychology of violence, I myself have learned of many comparable stories.

As I read these accounts I am struck by the innate ability of people to surmount at times the challenges of conflict and violence — and to use the rarely recognized human potential for overcoming violence without using it. We are shown here that there are forms of power we have been ignoring or downgrading for centuries, that physical force is not the last word in human affairs.

Some may perceive this power as psychological, others as spiritual. It is not necessary to agree on its origin to recognize that some sort of nonviolent energy was functioning through these individuals. We can see that there are ways to respond to violence that not only may halt the attack — but may even transform the hostility in the situation so as to replace an enemy with a friend.

In bringing out this first American edition, it is the publishers' goal to make available again a valuable source of historical and psychological data about human behavior in conflictual situations. We hope it contributes to the already growing interest and energy being devoted to finding different ways to deal with ancient problems — ways that are more effective, less violent and destructive, and have positive results that endure.

In further pursuit of this goal, I invite comments and questions about the book or the subjects of violence and conflict resolution. I am especially interested in additional true stories of similar nature (not necessarily as dramatic!). My research goes on with the hope of promoting greater understanding and use for these alternatives — through speaking and writing, and leading discussions in a variety of forums.

Jennifer Liberty Goodwin
Liberty Literary Works
1001 Atlantic Shores Blvd., #113
Hallandale, Florida 33009

If you wish to read more about dealing with violence and exploring its alternatives, I suggest these excellent books: *America Without Violence,* by Michael Nagler; *Courage in Both Hands,* by Alan Hunter; *Safe Passage on City Streets,* by Dorothy Samuels; *Strength to Love,* by Martin Luther King, Jr; *How to Live With—and Without—Anger,* by Albert Ellis; *What Would You Do?,* by John Yoder; and *Peace Pilgrim: Her Life and Work in Her Own Words* (also published by Ocean Tree Books).

CONTENTS

INTRODUCTION

IS THERE a practical alternative to the military system? Can disputes and difficulties, which we recognise as being fomented, rather than solved, by war, be dealt with satisfactorily by any other means? How can violence be met and overcome? In fact, is war necessary, or can it be eradicated?

These are some of the most important problems challenging thoughtful people to-day, upon which the fate of civilisation may almost be said to rest.

The pacifist maintains that war is not only utterly evil, but utterly useless, and that there is another and far better way— the conquest of evil by good, the opposing of spiritual power to physical violence, or so-called non-violent resistance. This volume does not attempt to explain or discuss this mysterious power, but merely to offer illustrations of its use under very varied circumstances: to show that dangerous situations have been safely passed through, and death or injury averted, without the use of material weapons, and to indicate that there exists a little-known sphere where exploration and experiment are badly needed, which offers a possibility of escape from the appalling threat to mankind so long as war continues.

The frequent taunt of the militarist to the pacifist, " Then you believe in doing nothing," may perhaps best be answered by showing the sort of action which the latter believes to be right, as an alternative to the militarist's belief in brute violence.

As for the pacifist technique here illustrated, it is hoped that it will be agreed that the following examples show that it needs courage and that it may claim success, although it should be added that there is no claim that such action would inevitably result in physical safety, or that physical safety is necessarily the highest good. But every incident which exemplifies the power of good to conquer evil and the fact that violence may be overcome without more violence, is an indication that there is a possible alternative to the futile crime of war.

For a full discussion of the subject, the reader is referred to " The Power of Non-Violence," by Richard Gregg.

A. R. F.

I place no hope whatever in force, no matter what form it takes. Nothing lifts us upward except the power which comes from within—science, invention, discovery, art, drama, morals, religion and exertion directed toward the supremest good. If these forces which issue forth from within are emitted, outward forces are powerless. My reliance is on the unseen inner forces.

KAGAWA.

Man, the brain, the boaster, the blind seeker,
Thrusting, merciless—and how much afraid!
Crouching behind his engines, still the weaker
For every tool of death his hands have made.

Man, the heart, the humble, the endurer,
Trusting, merciful, unafraid and gay,
Upright and free and friendly, still securer
For every warlike weapon thrown away.

W. R. HUGHES.

1. NON-RESISTANCE BY THE JEWS

" It was under the shadow of the coming storm (Babylonian Invasion) and the muttering of its distant thunder in their ears that the pious king (Josiah) and his ministers had laboured at the reformation by which they hoped to avert the threatened catastrophe. For with that unquestioning faith in the supernatural which was the strength, or the weakness, of Israel's attitude towards the world, they traced the national danger to national sin, and believed that the march of invading armies could be arrested by the suppression of heathen worship and a better regulation of the sacrificial ritual. Menaced by the extinction of their political independence, it apparently never occurred to them to betake themselves to those merely carnal weapons to which a less religious people would instinctively turn in such an emergency. To build fortresses, to strengthen the walls of Jerusalem, to arm and train the male population, to seek the aid of foreign allies—these were measures which to the gentile mind common sense might seem to dictate, but which to the Jew might appear to imply an impious distrust of Jehovah, who alone could save his people from their enemies."

Frazer, Folklore in the Old Testament, Vol. III, p. 108.

The above refers (in round figures) to 600 B.C. Due to this religious pacifist policy, the Jews—despite their present troubles—are still a *people* in the twentieth century A.D. Had they armed against the Babylonians they would have been not only conquered, but exterminated, for warfare in those days was more frank than it is now in its aims, and one might justifiably add, more thorough and less brutal in its methods.

The religious reformation of the period consisted in the condemnation and destruction of the " high places "—*i.e.,* the rural shrines on hill tops throughout the land whereat the Hebrew ritual had degenerated into heathen practices.

This is one of the earliest records of non-violent behaviour—the Exodus being in a different category—and it is very instructive, since its apparent failure then, proves a glorious triumph now. Had the Hebrews been slain instead of being led into captivity, civilisation would ultimately have been extinguished, for where is Babylon ? We should have had no Bible and no Christianity. The Chinese would doubtless have progressed, but their interest in the West would have ended when they had secured immunity from attack.

J. FRANKLYN.

2. " IF THINE ENEMY HUNGER "

During one of the wars between Israel and Syria, the King of Israel asked Elisha whether he should smite his enemies. Elisha answered : " Thou shalt not smite them : wouldst thou smite those whom thou hast taken captive with thy sword and with thy bow ? Set bread and water before them, that they may eat and drink, and go to their master." And he prepared great provision for them : and when they had eaten and drunk, he sent them away, and they went to their master. So the bands of Syria came no more into the land of Israel.

II Kings vi. 21-23.

3. THE POOR WISE MAN

This wisdom have I seen also under the sun, and it seemed great unto me : there was a little city, and few men within it ; and there came a great king against it, and besieged it, and built great bulwarks against it : now there was found in it a poor wise man, and he by his wisdom delivered the city ; yet no man remembered that same poor man. Then said I, Wisdom is better than strength : nevertheless the poor man's wisdom is despised, and his words are not heard. The words of wise men are heard in quiet more than the cry of him that ruleth among fools.

Wisdom is better than weapons of war : but one sinner destroyeth much good.

Ecclesiastes ix. 13-18.

4. PILATE AND THE ENSIGNS

Now, Pilate, the Procurator of Judea, removed the army from Cæsarea to Jerusalem, to take their winter-quarters there, in order to abolish the Jewish laws. So he introduced Cæsar's effigies, which were upon the ensigns, and brought them into the city ; whereas our Law forbids us the very making of images ; on which account the former Procurators were wont to make their entry into the city with such ensigns as had not those ornaments. Pilate was the first who brought these images to Jerusalem, and set them up there; which was done without the knowledge of the people, because it was done in the night-time; but as soon as they knew it, they came in multitudes to Cæsarea, and interceded with Pilate many days, that he would remove the images; and when he would not grant their requests, because it would tend to the injury of Cæsar, while yet they persevered in their request, on the sixth day he ordered his soldiers to have their weapons privately, while he came and sat upon his judgment-seat, which seat was so prepared in the open place of the city, that it concealed the army that lay ready to oppress them; and when the Jews petitioned him again, he gave a signal to the soldiers to encompass them round, and threatened that their punishment should be no less than immediate death, unless they would leave off disturbing him, and go their ways home. But they threw themselves upon the ground, and laid their necks bare, and said they would take their deaths very willingly, rather than the wisdom of their Laws should be transgressed; upon which Pilate was deeply affected with their firm resolution to keep their Laws inviolable, and presently commanded the images to be carried back from Jerusalem to Cæsarea.

Josephus', *Antiquities of the Jews*,
Bk. XVIII, Ch. iii.
(Whiston's translation)

5. THE MADNESS OF CÆSAR

Now Caius Cæsar did so grossly abuse the fortune he had arrived at, as to take himself to be a god, and to desire to be so called also, and to cut off those of the greatest nobility out of his country. He also extended his impiety as far as the Jews. Accordingly, he sent Petronius with an army to Jerusalem, to place his statues in the Temple, and commanded him that, in case the Jews would not admit of them, he should slay those that opposed it, and carry all the rest of the nation into captivity: but God concerned himself with these his commands. However, Petronius marched out of Antioch into Judæa, with three legions, and many Syrian auxiliaries. . . .

But now the Jews got together in great numbers, with their wives and children, into that plain that was by Ptolemais, and made supplication to Petronius, first for their Laws, and, in the next place, for themselves. So he was prevailed upon by the multitude of the supplicants, and by their supplications, and left his army and statues at Ptolemais, and then went forward into Galilee, and called together the multitude and all the men of note to Tiberias, and showed them the power of the Romans, and the threatenings of Cæsar; and, besides this, proved that their petition was unreasonable, because while all the nations in subjection to them had placed the images of Cæsar in their several cities, among the rest of their gods—for them alone to oppose it, was almost like the behaviour of revolters, and was injurious to Cæsar.

And when they insisted on their Law, and the custom of their country, and how it was not permitted them to make either an image of God, or indeed of a man, and to put it in any despicable part of their country, much less in the Temple itself, Petronius replied, " And am not I also," said he, " bound to keep the laws of my own lord? For if I transgress it, and spare you, it is but just that I perish; while he that sent me, and not I, will commence a war against you; for I am under command as well as you." Hereupon the multitude cried out, that they were ready to suffer for their law. Petronius then quieted them, and said to them, " Will you then make war against Cæsar? " The Jews said, " We offer sacrifices twice every day for Cæsar, and for the Roman people," but that if he would place the images among them, he must first sacrifice the whole Jewish nation; and that they were ready to expose themselves, together with their children and wives to be slain. At this Petronius was astonished, and pitied them on account of the inexpressible sense of religion the men were under, and that courage of theirs which made them ready to die for it; so they were dismissed without success.

. . . At last he got them together again, and told them that it was best for him to run some hazard himself; " for either, by the divine assistance, I shall prevail with Cæsar; and shall myself escape the danger as well as you, which will be matter of joy to us both; or, in case Cæsar continue in his rage, I will be ready to expose my own life for such a great number as you are." Whereupon he dismissed the multitude, who prayed greatly for his prosperity; and he took the army out of Ptolemais, and returned to Antioch; from whence he presently sent an epistle to Cæsar, and informed him of the irruption he had made into Judæa, and of the supplications of the nation; and that unless he had a mind to lose both the country and the men in it, he must permit them to keep their law, and must countermand his former injunction. Caius answered that epistle in a violent way, and threatened to have Petronius put to death for his being so tardy in the execution of what he had commanded. But it happened that those who brought Caius's epistle were tossed by a storm, and were detained on the sea three months, while others that brought the news of Caius's death had a good voyage. Accordingly, Petronius received the epistle concerning Caius, seven-and-twenty days before he received that which was against himself.

JOSEPHUS', *Wars of the Jews,*
Bk. II, Ch. x.
(Whiston's translation)

6. " COALS OF FIRE "

North of the Great Wall lies the land you rule over; south of that Wall are the families which are governed by me and are mine.

Let all peoples live in peace. Let parents and children never be divided. Let us try dismissing our troops, melting down our swords. Let us direct our efforts toward giving rest to the aged; let children grow up to manhood and all be joyous.

Your country lies far north, you will soon be suffering from the cold. I am having silk sent you, and cotton; rice and wheat. We are now friends; our peoples are glad; you and I are now more than their protectors; we are the parents of our peoples.

Let us reflect that the sky covers us all equally, the earth makes no distinction in bearing us; we are all one family.

Our wish is, that the world should be at peace for ever. Thus would the fish swim more tranquilly, the birds fly more freely; while the insects would hum their gladness in the heart of the woods.

Letter of the Emperor Wen-ti (born about 196 B.C.) *to the chief of the Hiong-nou, barbarians of the North who had broken their treaty with him and invaded his territory.*

7. WILLIAM CATON AND THE CROWD

William Caton, one of the early Friends, was confronted by a rude crowd, which marched up to his home in Sussex, beating a drum, and with obvious intent to do harm. He went to them and asked what they wanted. " Quakers," was the reply. " I am one," he said and fearlessly preached to them, so that they retired in fear and shame.

Early Annals of the Friends.

8. COL. CLIBBORN GIVES UP BURNING THE MEETING HOUSE

Colonel Clibborn was an officer in Cromwell's army. He had a great aversion to the Quakers, and " finding that they had a Meeting House on his land, in Ireland, he determined to clear them off by burning this house. Provided with fire he went to the place, supposing it to be empty ; but to his surprise, he found the meeting going on and Thomas Loe preaching. He threw away the fire and sat down behind the door, and became so powerfully affected that his purpose was immediately changed." Colonel Clibborn and his wife joined the Friends, but at this time Meetings were kept up at great hazard. His life was attempted three times. On one occasion, laying his head on a block, the hatchet was raised to strike the fatal blow. Colonel Clibborn called for a brief respite, and then kneeled down to pray that the sin might not be laid to their charge. Just then another party arrived, and asked, " Who have you there ? " and were answered, " Colonel Clibborn." The newcomers cried, " A hair of his head shall not be touched." He lived to see peace restored, and lived to a good old age.

Friends in Ireland,
by ALICE MARY HODGKIN, *Friends' Tract Association.*

9. THE " HOLY EXPERIMENT " OF WILLIAM PENN

The " Holy Experiment " of William Penn was a very remarkable example of the power of friendship without violence. Receiving the grant of a tract of land in America, nearly as large as England, from the King, Penn went there to rule over the Colonists and the Indians who lived there. By a treaty between him and his " subjects " the " only league between those nations and the Christians which was never sworn to and never broken " as Voltaire described it, Penn pledged himself to friendship and trust. This policy was so successful that " no drop of Quaker blood was ever shed by an Indian, no breach occurred for over seventy years, till the war party and the Church party at home succeeded in dispossessing the Quaker government of the Colony.

At the time of Penn's death, relations between Whites and Indians could hardly have been better, the frontier was safe from marauders, tomahawks and scalping knives were unknown, and traders were safe. There was much friendliness and hospitality between the two peoples and the Indians would take care of the little white children while their parents were at Meeting.

Unfortunately the sons and successors of William Penn did not maintain his high standard of conduct, and difficulties and failure naturally followed.

Thomas Chalkley, a Friend who visited the other Colonies early in the eighteenth century, tells that the Indians were " very barbarous in the destruction of the English inhabitants . . . but the great Lord of all was pleased wonderfully to preserve our Friends, especially those who kept faithful to their peaceable principle. . . . Among the many hundreds that were slain, I heard but of two or three of our Friends being killed, whose destruction was very remarkable, as I was informed (the one was a woman, the other two were men) the men used to go to their labour without any weapons, and trusted to the Almighty, and depended on His provision to protect them (it being their principle not to use weapons of war to offend others or to defend themselves). But a spirit of distrust taking place in their minds, they took weapons of war to defend themselves ; and the Indians who had seen them several times without them and let them alone, saying they were peaceable people and hurt nobody, therefore they would not hurt them, and now seeing them to have guns and supposing they designed to kill the Indians, they therefore shot the men dead."

One woman Friend was killed. She had lived in a lonely spot with her daughter and her family. At first she remained quietly there despite the danger ; but in time a " slavish fear " preyed upon her so that she induced her family to remove to a town where there was a garrison in which to take refuge. Her daughter, in an account which she left for her children, tells how her mother, after giving way to her fear, " found herself not at all easy but in a beclouded condition, and more shut from counsel than she had been since she knew the Truth, and being uneasy went to move to a Friend's house, that lived in the neighbourhood, and as she was moving, the bloody, cruel Indians lay by the way, and killed her. O then did I lament moving ! " The daughter and her husband moved back to the lonely home, where " we saw abundance of the wonderful works of the mighty power of the Lord, in keeping and preserving us when the Indians were at our doors and windows and at other times." Even when they went to Meeting, they left the children alone at home, and no harm came to them.

10. JOHN WESLEY FACES HIS ENEMIES

Thursday, 4th July, 1745.

" I rode to Falmouth. About three in the afternoon I went to see a gentlewoman who had been long indisposed. Almost as soon as I sat down, the house was beset on all sides by an innumerable multitude of people. A louder or more confused noise could hardly be at the taking of a city by storm. . . . The rabble roared with all their throats, ' Bring out the Canorum ! Where is the Canorum ? ' (an unmeaning word which the Cornish generally use instead of Methodist).[1]

" No answer being given, they quickly forced open the outer door, and filled the passage. Only a wainscot-partition was between us, which was not likely to stand long. I immediately took down a large looking-glass which hung against it, supposing the whole side would fall in at once. When they began their work with abundance of bitter imprecations, poor Kitty was utterly astonished, and cried out, ' O Sir, what must we do ? ' I said, ' We must pray.' Indeed, at that time, to all appearance, our lives were not worth an hour's purchase. She asked, ' But Sir, is it not better for you to hide yourself, to get into the closet ? ' I answered, ' No. It is best for me to stand just where I am.' Among those without were the crews of some privateers which were lately come into harbour. Some of these, being angry at the slowness of the rest, thrust them away, and, coming up all together, set their shoulders to the inner door, and cried out, ' Avast, lads, avast ! ' Away went all the hinges at once, and the door fell back into the room.

" I stepped forward at once into the midst of them, and said, ' Here I am. Which of you has anything to say to me ? To which of you have I done any wrong ? To you ? Or you ? ' I continued speaking till I came, bareheaded as I was (for I purposely left my hat that they might all see my face), into the middle of the street, and then raising my voice, said, ' Neighbours, countrymen ! Do you desire to hear me speak ? ' They cried vehemently, ' Yes, yes. He shall speak. He shall. Nobody shall hinder him.' But having nothing to stand on, and no advantage of ground, I could be heard by few only. However, I spoke without intermission and, as far as the sound reached, the people were still ; till one or two of their captains turned about and swore not a man should touch him."

John Wesley's Journal.

[1] Not really unmeaning, but old Cornish for one who sings or chants, and with the same antecedents as " cant "—A.R.F.

There were Methodist preachers in the eighteenth century who saw the full meaning of the teaching of Perfect Love in face of the wars with France. Outstanding was John Nelson. The Rules required Methodists to be "in every kind merciful after their power," to do "good of every possible sort, and as far as possible, to all men." John Nelson, seized by the press-gang for service in the army, applying the Christian ethic to war, refused to train as a soldier. Bullied, flung into foul dungeons, marched from town to town, he preached the full gospel of Christ to all who would listen.

Hear his story. At York, "A court-martial was held, and I was guarded to it by a file of musketeers, with their bayonets fixed. When I came before the court, they asked, 'What is this man's crime?' The answer was, 'This is the Methodist preacher, and he refuses to take money.' Then they turned to me, and said, 'Sir, you need not find fault with us, for we must obey orders, which are to make you act as a soldier; for you are delivered to us; and if you have not justice done you, we cannot help it.' My answer was, 'I shall not fight; for I cannot bow my knee before the Lord to pray for a man, and get up and kill him when I have done.' Next morning I was ordered to parade. The officers ordered Corporal W. to fetch me a gun and other war-like instruments. I asked, 'Why do you gird me with these war-like habiliments? for I am a man averse to war, and shall not fight, but under the Prince of Peace, the Captain of my salvation; and the weapons He gives me are not carnal like these.' At Sunderland the officers said they would make him wear clothing belonging to a soldier. Nelson answered, 'You may array me as a man of war, but I shall never fight.' They asked me, 'What is your reason?' My answer was, 'I cannot see anything in this world worth fighting for. I want neither its riches nor honours, but the honour that cometh from God only.'"

Nelson was finally discharged from the army, probably on the intervention of friends. To the major who set him at liberty he bore a parting Christian testimony. "Well," said the major, "if you be so scrupulous about fighting, what must we do?" I answered, "It is your trade; and if you had a better, it might be better for you." "But somebody," he replied, "must fight." I said, "If all men lived by faith in the Son of God, wars would be at an end." "That is true," he answered, "if it were so, we should learn war no more".

In the witness of John Nelson is the word for to-day. It derives directly from the Christ-given commandment of love; only by unqualified obedience to His bidding will war be vanquished.

From "*The Methodist. A Study in Discipleship,*"
by the REV. HENRY CARTER, C.B.E.

12. THE INDIANS COME TO MEETING

At the time of the fighting between England and her American Colonies in 1777, the neighbourhood of Easton, near New York, was so harassed by raids from both armies that the American Government advised evacuation of the people living there. But the Quakers remained and continued attendance at their Meetings. One weekday they were worshipping with open doors, when an Indian came and looked in, then quietly slipped in, followed by others. They put their weapons in a corner and sat down. Afterwards, one of the Friends invited them to a meal, after which they quietly went away. The chief warrior, who could speak French, said that they had come with the intention of killing all the Friends. "When we saw you sitting with your door open, without weapons of defence, we had no disposition to hurt you, we would have fought for you." So the scalping tomahawks they had brought with them were not used.

Quakers in Peace and War,
by M. HIRST, p. 390.

13. GUNPOWDER FALLS MEETING HOUSE

Robert Sutcliffe records, "During the revolutionary war in America, a part of the American army lay near Gunpowder Falls Meeting House, which, however, did not prevent Friends from holding their Meetings for worship. Amongst the troops there was a colonel of dragoons whose hatred of Friends was raised to such a pitch of malice that one day when traversing the country, he came to the most cruel and extraordinary resolution of putting to the sword the Friends who were then collected at their places of worship, considering them as no better than a company of traitors. Drawing up his men near the spot, he ordered them to halt in order to make arrangements for the execution of his dreadful purpose. At this moment an awful silent pause took place in which he felt his mind so powerfully smitten with conviction that he not only drew off his men, but conceived very favourable sentiments of the Society he finally joined."

Incidents and Reflections,
F. WALTON.

14. WILLING TO BE PLUNDERED

There was much suffering on the island of Nantucket during the Revolutionary War, unable as they were to pursue their usual whaling industry. Also they were liable to plunder from privateers who could only gain access to their one harbour while the wind was from the west; and on several occasions they had been prevented from entering by long-continued easterly winds. But now Providence seemed to have forsaken them, for a vessel flying English colours anchored where she could command the town with her guns. A boat was seen to put off from her and divers of the inhabitants were gathered on the wharf in anxious expectation. As an officer stepped ashore William Rotch, a prominent Friend offered him his hand and said, " I would like thee to come to my house." This was a different reception from what had been expected ; but supposing him to be a loyalist the officer went, it being near noon. William said, " I would like thee to take dinner with me." After it was over the officer, feeling that he must be about the business he was sent on, said, " I came here for plunder and I would like you to tell me, as a friend, how and where I had better begin." William said, " I don't know any better place for thee to begin than here at my house, for I am better able to bear the loss than anyone else." Looking at him curiously, " Are there any more men like you on this island ? " " Yes, there are many better men that I am here." " I should like to see some of them." " Well, I will introduce thee to some of our leading citizens." Going into a store he said, " This man distributed 400 barrels of flour among the poor of the island last winter." After talking a while he was taken to another store and told of something similar that man had done. On leaving, the officer entended his hand to William saying, " Farewell." He put off to the ship, she weighed anchor and that was the last they saw of her.

HOWARD T. JONES,
Iowa.

15. ABBY GREENE AND THE SOLDIERS

Abby Greene, a Quaker woman whose husband was a sympathiser with the American " rebellion ", knew that the British soldiers had been ordered to burn down her house. Persuading her excitable husband to leave the matter to her, she welcomed the officer at her door with, " I hope you have not come to do us any harm ? Come in, I will get you something to eat." After a moment's pause, the officer replied, " Dear old mother, we won't hurt a hair of your head." He stamped out the brand in his hand, and with all his men accepted her invitation to tea.

Quakers in the Forum,
by AMELIA GUMMERE.

16. SHAKERS PROTECTED BY THEIR FRIEND, THE GUERILLA LEADER

During the plundering, raiding, violent border struggles of the Civil War the Shakers of Pleasant Hill, in Kentucky, dwelt in peace and security under the powerful protection of a most " unlooked-for protector, no less a personage than the notorious guerilla leader, John Morgan." It appears that Morgan had grown up in the vicinity of the Shaker community, and cherished a profound respect for those quiet, kindly people. Hence, when the Confederate foragers were hatching a design against the well-stored Shaker larders and barns, he peremptorily forbade the foray. He then informed his troops that he had known the Shakers from long acquaintance, as " a harmless, inoffensive people ; that they took no part with either side, injured no man and had no desire to do so, and none under his command should injure them in any way."

Shakerism, Its Meaning and Message,
by WHITE AND TAYLOR.
Quoted in *Non-Violent Coercion,*
by C. M. CASE.

17. ABRAHAM SHACKLETON

I understand only one young man of our Society has fallen and that by his imprudence joining the Army and was shot by the opposite party. Some Friends' houses have been burned and their property. This place remains quiet as to any inroad of an outward enemy but fears abound in general among the inhabitants. A. Shackleton was taken by the Insurgents and was with them two days and three nights.

They wanted him to head them but on his refusing, after many threats, they let him go on condition that he would try to make peace on as good terms as he could for them when the two armies

were in sight of each other—which he affected without the loss
of a Life, by their laying down their arms, etc.

*Extract from letter from Edward Hatton to John
Eliot, Cork, 13, vi. 1798 (during the Civil War in
Ireland). From " The Eliot Papers," by Eliot
Howard. Pub. by E. Hicks. 1895.*

18

Archbishop Sharpe was assaulted by a footpad on the highway,
who presented a pistol and demanded his money. The Archbishop spoke to the robber in the language of a fellow-man and of
a Christian. The man was really in distress, and the prelate gave
him such money as he had, and promised that, if he would call
at the palace, he would make up the amount to fifty pounds.
This was the sum of which the robber had said he stood in the
utmost need. The man called and received the money. About a
year and a half afterwards, this man again came to the palace
and brought back the same sum. He said that his circumstances
had become improved, and that, through the " astonishing good-
ness " of the Archbishop he had become " the most penitent, the
most grateful, and happiest of his species." Let the reader consider how different the Archbishop's feeling were, from what
they would have been if by his hand, this man had been cut off.

From *Principles of Morality,*
by JONATHAN DYMOND (1796-1828).

19. ELIZABETH FRY ENTERS PRISON

On a cold January day in 1817, in the gloomy vestibule outside
the women's yard at Newgate, two turnkeys might have been
seen arguing with a lady. The row inside the yard was as great
as usual. Even while they talked a woman rushed wildly out
of a doorway and, with shrieks of furious laughter, snatched off
the caps and headgear of every woman that she could reach.
" And she wouldn't stop at doing that to you, ma'am. Tear off
your things—scratch and claw you—that's what they'd do, ma'am."
The turnkeys felt that delicacy forbade telling all that could be
done by these harridans to a lady who ventured alone into their
midst. They themselves knew better than to go in alone ; they
always went in two together. The Governor himself went in
guarded. But the lady was obstinate. She had in her hand a
powerful permit from the prison Governor. She smiled, and
gave the men a little money. But she talked to them with an

unconscious authority, as she would have talked to her gardeners at home. " I am going in—and alone. I thank you for your kind intentions, but you are not to come with me," was the purport of her speech. At least, then, she must leave her watch behind. They could see the glittering chain on the quiet richness of her Quaker dress. But the unreasonable lady would not even do that ! " Oh, no, I thank you. My watch goes with me everywhere. I am not afraid ! Open the gate for me, please ! "

Reluctant, sullen, and very much alarmed as to the results, the turnkeys pressed open the gate against the begging, scuffling crowd, and Elizabeth Fry went in. The gate clanged and locked behind her. There was an instantaneous silence of sheer astonishment. Then every woman in the yard surged forward. Curiosity can be as dangerous as violence in a rough crowd. The lady was surrounded—the turnkeys could only see the tip of her white cap. But no one was snatching. Now was seen one benefit of Quaker dress : it was not provocative. There were no feathers, no flying fancy scarves, to tempt a mischievous finger or an unsatisfied cupidity. And the Quaker dress was an outward and visible mark of religion. All these wicked women, as the Newgate prisoner had said, respected religion and believed in God. Yet Elizabeth was in great danger. If she should now show fear, or say or do the wrong thing—But she had never been less afraid in her life. Look what is she doing now ? She has picked up a filthy little child, and it can be seen fingering her bright chain. She lifts her hand for attention, and she is attended to.

" Friends, many of you are mothers. I too am a mother. I am distressed for your children. Is there not something we can do for these innocent little ones ? Do you want them to grow up to become real prisoners themselves ? Are they to learn to be thieves and worse ? . . . "

Ah, she has touched the spot. She has pierced their armour to the very heart. What, save their children ? Sobs and tears answered her appeal. They gave her a chair, and brought their children to show her. What tales they told in their inarticulate way, of wickedness, remorse, injustice, and despair ! She remained with them for hours.

And when at last she bade them farewell, and the barred gate opened for her civil egress, she left behind her an inhabitant very strange to Newgate, one usually as much abandoned at its doors as at the very gate of Hell, that reviving spirit of human vitality called Hope.

From *Life of Elizabeth Fry,*
by JANET WHITNEY.

20. ELIZABETH FRY AND THE BURGLAR

Elizabeth Fry was staying at a Hotel in Bristol, for the purpose of her prison work, when she saw a man's boot protuding from under the bed. She knelt down by it and prayed aloud for the burglar, who soon crept out and joined her. At the end she asked him, " And now friend tell me what brought thee hither ? " His story was of starvation driving him to steal for the first time, a story she verified and followed up with adequate help. She had to escort him to the door to prevent his being stopped by the porter.

From *The Howard Journal,* 1925, p. 220.

21. THE SAFETY OF THE UNARMED CONSCIENTIOUS OBJECTORS

In the Civil War in America many conscientious objectors refused to become soldiers. For instance, Isaiah Macon was arrested by the military authorities and hurried to the army in the Valley of Virginia.

The battle of Winchester occurred immediately afterwards, and the officers said, " If Macon will not fight put him in front to stop bullets for those who will." Hemmed in by the soldiers he could not escape if he would. His comrades were falling all round him from the leaden hail of the northern soldiers. But he stopped no bullets, seeming to bear a charmed life, for his comrades fell all round him, their places being filled by others who wondered at the strange sight—a man with plain citizen's dress, having neither pistol, sword, nor gun, and no military cap nor coat, calmly filling his place in battle line, but taking no part in battle.

When retreat was ordered, he calmly lay down on the ground, and was taken prisoner by the advancing Northern army. He died a few days afterwards, probably from shock.

Another objector, William Hockett, wrote, " They were ordered by Colonel Kirkland to ' Load, present arms : Aim,' and their guns were pointed at my breast. I raised my arms and prayed, ' Father forgive them for they know not what they do.' Not a gun was fired. An officer then swore he would ride over me, and made every effort to do so, but failed, for his horse could not be made to step on me."

Yet another young American, Lazarus Pearson, was surrounded in his own home by a mob, telling him to recant from refusal to fight. They brought a rope to hang him, which he told them to do publicly, where all could see. At least one hundred men gathered round him. Then someone cried, " We ought not to hang so good a citizen as he." Dissension broke out and finally all left him except two young men to whom he had been kind years before, who said they would have died with him, rather than see him hanged.

These are only illustrations of many similar experiences.

Southern Heroes. Cartland.

22. FRIENDS IN THE IRISH REBELLION

Mary Leadbeter

Mary Leadbeter, an Irish Quaker, who writes of her terrible experiences in the Irish Rebellion of 1798 relates how the peaceable inhabitants of her home town of Ballitore " were delivered up for two hours to the unbridled licence of a furious soldiery." Soldiers poured into her house, rudely demanding food. One man, she writes, " cursed me with great bitterness, and, raising his musket, presented it to my breast. I desired him not to shoot me. It seemed as if he had the will, but not the power to do so. He turned from me, dashed pans and jugs off the kitchen table with his musket, and shattered the kitchen window."

The Annals of Ballitore,

by Mary Leadbeter.

Dinah Goff

Dinah Goff, an Irish Friend, narrated her experiences at fourteen years of age. She was one of the twenty-two children of Jacob and Elizabeth Goff of Horetown, Co. Wexford, where the disturbances were the greatest. Their house was between two rebel camps, whose officers ransacked their stores of food and took their horses, and on one occasion a violent battle raged for three hours round the house, cannon-balls falling thickly about it while the Goffs waited, terrified, upstairs. Next morning when many of the officers breakfasted with them, they saw that cannon had been pointed against the house to batter it down, but as the match was lighted, a man who knew Jacob Goff said that it was a Quakers' not a rebel house, and it was saved.

Every day hundreds of refugees and rebels were fed, on the

lawn, from tubs of milk and water and quantities of bread and cheese. While Dinah and her sisters attended to the unwelcome guests, they told gruesome stories of the cruelties they enacted. One day a number of soldiers appeared on the lawn, carrying a black flag, which they knew to be a signal for death.   Jacob Goff and his wife advanced fearlessly, and the soldiers prepared their muskets for firing.   One looked to another and said, " Why don't you begin ? " and the muttered answer came, " We cannot." So, " unprotected," they were saved.

After the rebellion was over their experiences were almost more terrifying, for the house was entered at night by a mob of armed men demanding money, and when given all there was, insisted that they must have more or they would kill Jacob Goff.   Poor Dinah, sleeping in an inner room, rushed in to see a man about to kill her father with drawn sword, which was just intercepted by her elder sister. Again the ruffians threatened Goff, and this time Dinah clung desperately to her father though told she would be killed.   Her father replied that she would rather be hurt if he were, and though pistols were fired, eventually the unarmed family were left uninjured.

Divine Protection through Extraordinary Dangers,

DINAH W. GOFF, 1857.

JOSEPH HAUGHTON

Joseph Haughton, a Friend, writing in 1811, tells of the awful experiences of the rebellion in Ireland in 1798, and " how much better it is to put our trust in the Lord than to put confidence in princes : and to keep faithful to the truth as it is revealed in the mind is a far more sure defence than all the efforts human policy can make or procure."

The Friends were concerned that all of their members who had guns in their houses for domestic purposes should destroy them and Joseph Haughton took his fowling piece, " and broke it in the street opposite my own house, which was a matter of wonder amongst my neighbours." For this reason the houses of Quakers were left unmolested, when arms were searched for.

J. Haughton, writing of the danger from the soldiers, " Some of them came to my house one morning, and told me that my place was to be burned that day in consequence of my having refused to turn out the Protestant women who were sheltering there.   I told them if they could do so I could not help it, but that as long as I had a house I would keep it open to succour the distressed, and if they burned it for my so doing, I should only have to turn out along with the others and share their affliction. It was our Meeting day, and with a heavy heart I took my family to Meeting about a mile distant, and expected on my return to find ourselves bereft of a habitation and even of a substance. But the good hand that had hitherto preserved us did not permit them to fulfil their threat; nor did they, that I remember, require the like afterwards. I found that the more I attended to what was right in my own mind, the more I seemed to be respected by them. Even when I have expostulated with them concerning the cruelties committed by them at their camps, particularly at Vinegar Hill and at Wexford, also their burning men and women in the barn of Scullabogue, they have quietly listened to my remonstrance and frequently acknowledged the wrong.

"The only Friend known to have been killed in those troublous times was a young man near Rathangan, who sought for safety among the king's army, and fell a victim to party rage.

"Strangers passing the houses of Friends, and seeing them preserved, with ruins on either hand, would frequently, without knowledge of the district, say they were Quakers' houses."

JOSEPH HAUGHTON'S *God's Protecting Providence*, in *Friends in Ireland*.

23. THE HUNGARIAN STRIKE

The Emperor Franz Josef was trying to subordinate Hungary to the Austrian power, contrary to the terms of the old treaty of union between the two countries. The Hungarian moderates felt helpless, as they were too weak to fight. But Francis Deak, a Catholic landowner of Hungary, protested to them—"Your laws are violated, yet your mouths remain closed. Woe to the nation which raises no protest when its rights are outraged! It contributes to its own slavery by its silence. The nation which submits to injustice and oppression without protest is doomed."

Deak proceeded to organise a scheme for independent Hungarian education, agriculture and industry, a refusal to recognise the Austrian Government in any way, and a boycott against Austrian goods, He admonished the people not to be betrayed into acts of violence, nor to abandon the ground of legality. "This is the safe ground," he said, "on which, unarmed ourselves, we can hold our own against armed force. If suffering must be necessary, suffer with dignity." This advice was obeyed throughout Hungary.

When the Austrian Tax collector came, the people did not beat him or even hoot at him—they merely declined to pay. The Austrian police then seized their goods, but no Hungarian auctioneer would sell them. When an Austrian auctioneer was brought, he found that he would have to bring bidders from Austria to buy the goods. The government soon found that it was costing more to distrain the property than the tax was worth.

The Austrians attempted to billet their soldiers upon the Hungarians. The Hungarians did not actively resist the order, but the Austrian soldiers, after trying to live in houses where everyone despised them, protested strongly against it. The Austrian Government declared the boycott of Austrian goods illegal, but the Hungarians defied the decree. The jails were filled to overflowing. No representatives from Hungary would sit in the Imperial Parliament.

The Austrians then tried conciliation. The prisoners were released and partial self-government given. But Hungary insisted upon the full claims. In reply, Emperor Franz Josef decreed compulsory military service. The Hungarians answered that they would refuse to obey it. Finally, on February 18th, 1867, the Emperor capitulated and gave Hungary her Constitution.

The Power of Non-Violence,

by RICHARD GREGG.

24. MARY SLESSOR OF CALABAR

Mary Slessor (b. 1848) was the child of a drunken shoemaker, who began to work in a textile factory at the age of eleven. When quite young she began to teach in a mission, and braved the danger of outdoor speaking which was likely to be molested by roughs. One night the mob leader swung a leaden weight at the end of a cord, nearer and nearer to Mary's head, shaving her brow. She never winced. " She' s game, boys," cried her tormentor, and he and his followers attended her Meeting.

At the age of 28 she sailed as a Missionary to Calabar, and settled amongst the exceedingly fierce tribe of Okoyong, who practiced many terribly fierce and cruel customs. At Creek Town everyone said her task was hopeless, but undeterred she walked thither through the dark forest nearly sobbing and longing to run away from her difficult task. She was accompanied by a Scotchman and four black children whom she had adopted. On one occasion the son of a chief was killed by an accident and Mary Slessor knew that human sacrifices would follow.

Witchcraft indicated a certain village as guilty and about a dozen prisoners, including three women with their babies, were brought from it, and the people became frenzied with mad delight. Mary determined to watch ceaselessly by the prisoners—her vigil shared by her Scotch companion, while the wild people, half naked and armed with guns, danced and drank endless rum. She helped one woman to escape and the chiefs released some others to please her, and finally she managed to save all.

On another occasion a brother of the chief determined to take the poison ordeal to show the falsehood of a rumour that he had killed his nephew. Mary Slessor made him promise not to, and claimed the poison beans as guarantee. He denied having any, but she found them, and carried them to her hut. Before long, hearing shouting, she went back and found that, mad with drink, the chief was clinging to the bag of beans. Quietly, persistently, Mary demanded the bag, and he threw it at her, and she found forty beans at the bottom. " I'll take the liberty of keeping these," she said, calmly. " No, no," he shouted. Outwardly calm, this woman who at home was so shy she could not speak before men if she could see them, walked through lines of armed men, ironically bidding them take the bag from her. But their hands were held, and she passed safely through.

Once Mary Slessor prevented two tribes from fighting each other. With heart beating wildly, she stood between them, and made each group pile their guns on either side of her, till the piles were 5 ft. high.

Another similar achievement was when she needed furlough badly, but just as she was preparing to go, she heard of an imminent war. Against all advice, she insisted on going to the place. Reaching the village at midnight she sent a message to the chief at once. The chief replied diplomatically that he knew of no war, but if there were, Mary was showing her ignorance of the people, who were warlike and not likely to be helped by a woman. To which her answer was, " In measuring the woman's power, you have evidently forgotten to take into account the woman's God." After various adventures she reached the centre of the war-fever, and war preparations. Speaking as if to schoolboys, she told the people to keep the peace and not to behave like fools. When she met a solid wall of armed men, who would make no reply to her, an old chief, whom she had once cured, suddenly stepped out and knelt at her feet, admitting the wounding of the enemy chief and begging her to use her influence for peace with the other side. She told them to wait till she had eaten and they had found a good place for her to confer with two or three men of good judgment on both sides. Mary knelt and begged for magnanimity and arbitration instead of war. It was agreed, and although a few hours of frenzy followed, urging the "manlier" way of war, a fine was finally paid and a promise given to keep the peace while Mary was on furlough, which was faithfully adhered to.

Never was she in any way molested, though once accidentally struck in a brawl. Both sides would have killed the offender had Mary not saved him. The Government allowed her to go her own way, dealing out real justice, surrounded by her "ladies and babies in waiting."

Mary Slessor of Calabar,
by W. P. LIVINGSTONE.

25. MOSHEU, THE AFRICAN CHIEF

Robert Moffat, the Scottish missionary in Africa, records a remarkable incident among native Christians. A group of them were scarcely seated at a prayer-meeting one Sunday when a party of marauders approached and having failed in plundering elsewhere, were determined to attack this village. Mosheu, the chief, arose, and begged the people to sit still and trust in Jehovah, while he went to meet the marauders. To his inquiry what they wanted, the appalling reply was, "Your cattle, and it is at your peril you raise a weapon to resist." "There are my cattle," replied the chief, and then retired and resumed his position at the prayer-meeting. A hymn was sung, a chapter read, and then all kneeled in prayer to God, Who only could save them in their distress. The sight was too sacred and solemn to be gazed at by such a band of ruffians; they all withdrew from the spot without touching a single article belonging to the people.

Missionary Labours and Scenes in Southern Africa,
by ROBERT MOFFAT.

26. THE ROWDIES RESPECTED HER

On a memorable occasion, when the Annual Meeting of the Anti-Slavery Society in New York (at which John G. Whittier and William Lloyd Garrison were present) was broken up by rowdies, some of the speakers, as they left the hall, were roughly handled by the crowd. Perceiving this, Lucretia Mott asked the gentleman who was escorting her, to leave her and help some of the other ladies who were timid. " But who will take care of you ? " said he. " This man," she answered, quietly laying her hand on the arm of one of the roughest of the mob ; " he will see me safe through." Though taken aback for the moment by such unexpected confidence, the man responded by conducting her respectfully through the tumult to a place of safety. The next day she went into a restaurant near by the place of meeting, and, recognising the leader of the mob at one of the tables, sat down by him, and entered into conversation with him. When he left the room, he asked a gentleman at the door who that lady was, and on hearing her name, remarked, " Well, she's a good, sensible woman."

Life and Letters,
JAMES AND LUCRETIA MOTT.

27. AN ADVENTURE WITH THE KU KLUX KLAN

In the early summer of 1869 I was engaged as an engineer on construction on a railroad controlled by one of the Southern State Governments.

Being a Quaker I was strongly advised by the chief Engineer to say nothing about Quakerism, or the abolition of Slavery (the latter recently effected by the war).

He said that all the Quakers had been run out of that State in consequence of their protests against Slavery, and their systematic assistance given to escaping slaves, that some of the last to go had had their houses and barns destroyed, and had been stripped, tarred and feathered, " ridden on a rail " and thrown into the nearest river. He added that the citizens had generally made a vow that if any Quaker again entered the State they would make it hot for him.

I was directed to go to the town of A—, to wait there till the engineering corps assembled, and was given an introduction to General H—, President of the Railway, who resided in the town ; I called on him. He invited me to a ball he was giving in a few days' time in the College buildings.

The next day, it being very hot, I arranged with a gentleman whose acquaintance I had made, to go with him at dusk to bathe in a mill pond about two miles off.

Returning, and when a quarter of a mile from the boarding-house, at a junction of two roads, we saw in the bright moonlight, a man on horseback, both man and horse entirely covered with calico except holes for eyes, mouth and nose.

He motioned us to go the other way (which would take us about a mile round). My companion at once obeyed, and tried to get me to do so too. I refused, and walked on, when the man drew his pistol and cocked it at me.

That settled the question, and when we were some little distance along the roundabout road, I asked my companion what it meant.

He seemed not to understand.

" Why ! " I said, " that masquerading man on horse-back who threatened to shoot me."

" There was no such man ; you must be dreaming."

As I insisted on it, he looked round, and then replied in a low voice :

" As you value your life, you have seen no such thing, and you must not mention it again."

Coming into the town, we met two acquaintances. I asked the same question. They both looked queer and said :

" You must have been dreaming," and advised me strongly not to say a word on the subject. My landlady, when appealed to, also looked round apprehensively, and then said, " You've mistaken something in the moonlight " : and when I insisted she said, " It is very dangerous to talk of such things : don't do it any more." I said I would ask every person I met till I got at the truth. She then told me it was a sentinel of the Ku Klux Klan, and as there was another near her house, they were evidently doing some business between the two places, but it was very dangerous to talk of such things. Next day it was stated that a prominent negro, a blacksmith, residing on that short piece of road, had " left the country," and I heard people speaking in pitying tones of his " widow ". I soon found there was a perfect reign of terror there, but no one would give evidence ; even the widow would not say anything, and neither she nor her children would reply when questioned.

The oath which all the Klu Klux took, as was afterwards ascertained at the State inquiry, was, that they would stop short of no crime to maintain the supremacy of the white race, and that if ordered to do so by the Council, they would kill their nearest and dearest relatives and friends, and would pursue to the death anyone who betrayed a secret of the Klan, or gave evidence against the Order.

I went to the ball, and not being a dancer, I was conversing with Miss H—, daughter of the General, and others in a side room opening out of the dancing hall. They began talking of the abolition of slavery. I " laid low ". Presently Miss H—said,

"If there is one set of people on earth for whom I have unmitigated horror, loathing and contempt, it is the Quaker Abolitionists of England, who, safe enough themselves, egged on and helped their co-religionists on this side."

" Mr. T—, you have not said a word on the subject. As a Northern man, what do you think of them ? " I replied, " Miss H—, after your last remark it is very difficult for me to reply, as I am an English Quaker Abolitionist."

Miss H— coloured up and a young gentleman standing by said to her, in the awkward pause that ensued :

" I have been asked by the General to take you down to the supper room."

I asked a young lady who had taken the side of the North in the conversation if I might escort her down ; she consented, but said :

" Let me tell you after your avowal to Miss H—I am the only lady in this entire gathering who would take your arm, and I tell you as a friend you had better leave the State by next morning train, as they won't have Quakers here."

After supper, I was standing by myself when, as if by pre-concert, the group I had been with gathered round me, and Miss H— gave a very graceful apology, saying she had no idea I was either an Englishman, a Quaker, or an Abolitionist, or she never would have made the remark she did.

The young man who had taken her down to supper then said that he had lived all his life in that part, and had never heard the Quakers spoken of except in terms of opprobrium, so there was some excuse for Miss H—, and now that they had a real live one with them, they would like me to give them the other side of the question.

" With great pleasure."

" Then we will give you a hearing," said a deep strong voice behind me. It was the General.

Just then a dance came to an end, and General H—announced that they had with them an English Quaker Abolitionist, who would now give them in a speech, not exceeding a quarter of an hour, a defence of his people ; the dancing in the meantime would be stopped, and he should consider it as a personal affront to *himself* if anyone interrupted the speaker.

" Now Mr. T—, go up into the rostrum."

I went up, and my position, looking down on the assembly, gave me confidence. When I had finished and sat down there was some slight pause.

During the next hour three gentlemen who had given me

invitations to social functions, came and cancelled them, and till the day I left the town of — some months after, I never entered the house of a citizen of the State as a guest. Next day, no one seemed to care to be seen in my company, or to speak to me. But the following morning three gentlemen came to me, and said they were sent by a very important Society, to know exactly what my opinions on slavery were. I said that if they were at the ball (and I thought I had seen them there) they had already got what they wanted. They said that would not do, they were representing a very important Society, and must take down the information direct. Then I said " you may tell your very important Society to mind their own business, and I will mind mine."

After lunch as I went into my room, I saw pinned on my wooden window sill a letter directed to myself, as follows :

A skull and crossbones were depicted on one side, a railway train on the other, and in the centre was written, " You are required to leave the State within 24 hours or we will not be responsible for your life."

By order of the Council,—K.K.K.

I asked two or three gentlemen whom I knew, if they thought it was a hoax. They replied,

" We know it is not a hoax, and if you do not leave by the night train there is hardly a white man in the country who will not be bound by his oath to kill you."

This was pleasant, I had just got a splendid situation, exactly what I wanted, and did not wish to lose it. I felt, too, that if I went off they would say :

" These cowardly Quakers, they won't fight, but they will run away fast enough," and the more I thought of it, and the more I prayed over it, the stronger the conviction came that I *must* fight it out. I went up to my room and sat down seeking to be directed aright. Almost immediately I felt it strongly laid upon me not to waste a second, but to go at once, and publicly defy the Ku Klux Klan in the Town Square.

I hurried to the Square, and on the opposite side, directly in front of the Post Office, I saw a high barrel on end, and two boxes for steps leading to it. I at once mounted it and waving the letter, attracted a crowd. Just then thirteen or fourteen men in " tall hats " (I had seen no tall hats there before) came out of the Post Office and were making for the hotel when they saw me, turned back and listened, while I made a speech as nearly as possible as follows :

"Gentlemen, I have heard a great deal about Southern Hospitality and Southern Chivalry, but ninety-nine hundredths of what I have heard has been from yourselves since my coming down here. The constant reiteration has almost sickened me, and has made me wonder what it meant, and now I have learned. I came down here at the request of some of your most eminent citizens, to plan out your Railway, intending to mind my own business and not to interfere with any of your institutions, especially slavery. Slavery is a 'dead horse' and it is no use whipping it. Yet because, at the request of a lady, and of General H—, who is virtually my employer, I gave my opinions on that subject, I am ordered to leave the State within twenty-four hours or be murdered."

I then read and exhibited the letter.

"Now if there are any Ku Klux here present (and I am quite sure there are), I wish them to give my replies to their Council. I will *not* leave the State within twenty-four hours, but to-night at 8 o'clock, unarmed as I always am, I will go outside the town and round the Lutheran Church, which is the most lonely place I can think of, and if any Ku Klux like to meet me then they can." The thirteen men in tall hats walked off and several people warned me I was going "to my grave." At 3 p.m. J.H.—, the son of the General, called with a letter from his father, saying I *must* leave by the night train, and that an escort would be at my lodgings and would take me to the station, and General H— would guarantee safe conduct to beyond the confines of the State, and would give me a free pass. I thanked him but said I was going to fight it out. He said it was absolute suicide; but finding persuasion of no avail, he left me.

Too nervous to eat any supper, I got so weak and trembling by 7.45 that I felt I could hardly walk. Opening the door, I found J.H.—, the General's son, and a knot of young men, who said they had come to take me to the Station, and had got a free pass. My landlady, and a lot of the crowd urged me to go with them, but I declined, and went in the other direction. Not a soul followed. It was pitch dark, as there was no moon; it was cloudy, and I had to feel my way by the corners of the fence. I began to think what I should say, when the text seemed given me—

"If you are brought before rulers and kings, take no thought what ye shall say, for it shall be told you in that hour what you ought to say." (The substance of *Luke* xxi. 12).

So I thought no more about it, and felt strengthened and encouraged. When three-quarters round the Church a voice said:

"Halt! Who goes there?"

I replied.

Several men surrounded me. The following conversation took place.

"What do you mean by defying the Ku Klux Klan?"

"What do you mean by ordering me to leave the State? Have I not just as much right here as you have?"

They, seeming surprised and nonplussed at my answer, said:

"We know perfectly well who you are, a spy of the State Governor, pretending to be an Engineer of the Railway."

"I am no spy, and did not know the name of the Governor till seeing the proclamation on the wall of the Court House to-day. I have my credentials in my hand, and will hand them to you if you will promise to give them back."

"Promise to give them back!" and they seized hold of them. All but one then went off to read them. The one man who remained, cocked his pistol, put it to my head, so that I could feel the cold steel, and said:

"You are a dead man if you move."

"Do you mind my sitting down on this gravestone, as I am rather faint?"

"No"—and muttered, "nor *underneath* it".

They were a very long time gone and the man who was standing over me was constantly clicking his pistol, and feeling me with his foot to see if I was still there. It was very dark.

At last the others arrived and took away the first man, while a second stood over me. Then they returned, said my credentials clearly supported my statement, and if I would agree to leave next day, they would let me off.

I declined.

They conferred again, and then said:

"We don't want to execute you, and will let you off if you will make a public recantation of Quakerism and abolitionism to-morrow in the same place where you read our letter.

I declined this.

They conferred again, then asked me what I would propose.

I said I had come there determined not to interfere with their institutions, that Slavery was dead, and it had not been my intention to say anything about it, but this was a free country or ought to be so, and if I was asked my opinions as I *was* asked at the ball, I should give them.

They conferred again.

I felt they were quite as anxious as I was for some *modus vivendi*.

" Will you promise not to run for a political office such as postmaster or senator ? "

I promised, but reminded them that Engineer of the State-controlled Railway came very near.

" Oh ! we don't mind that, that's scientific."

" Will you promise not to raise or assist in raising any insurrection among the negroes ? "

I told them they knew very little about Quakerism as such an idea was utterly contrary to our principles.

" Well, will you promise not to attend negro meetings ? "

" I attended the negro political meeting last night from curiosity, but the air was so bad it would, in any case, be a long time before I should care to attend another," and I promised.

" Then give us back our letter in exchange for your credentials."

They shook hands and said I could go, and that so long as I kept my word I should be quite safe from the K.K.K.

I went back, and next day was in a high fever.

No one ever asked me what had happened.

Some months later an eminent negro minister came to the town and advertised a meeting for worship. I attended. Next day a letter came.

" You have broken your promise.—K.K.K."

I immediately went into the square, made a speech opposite the Post Office to a small crowd, reading the letter and saying I thought my promise only referred to a *political* meeting, but seeing they took it the other way, I should consider it as they understood it to have been.

Soon after " the bottom fell out ".

A rumour got abroad that people were betraying the K.K.K. and in panic, crowds of men besieged the offices of the Justices of the Peace all over the country, to make depositions in the hope of being made States' Evidence, and thus saving their own necks. It then appeared that almost every White man in the State (including General H— and his son, who had joined from fear of their lives) were members of the Klan. Almost every one was constructively a murderer, as whenever it was decided to murder anyone, ten or twelve " lodges " were each required to send ten or twelve men to assist at the work, surround the place and take out the man and kill him by burning, hanging or shooting. An amnesty was passed, and everybody was, or pretended to be, intensely relieved that the Ku Klux Klan was dead.

Soon after this the Governor told me that within half-an-hour of my giving defiance, he knew all about it and was delighted, as he took it for granted I should be murdered, and he could prove this murder, and so would be able to proclaim martial law.

"Do you know," said he, "what saved you?"

"No."

"Did you see about a dozen men with tall hats and with staves?"

"Yes."

"They were the Radical Committee of the Western Division of the State, and the K.K.K. knew that those men would tell me, and assist in proving the murder, and I could nearly have torn my hair with vexation when I heard next morning you had got off. But for those men coming out *when they did,* your life would not have been worth a cent."

The above incident was noised all over the neighbouring States, and wherever I went I was known as "the Quaker" and as "the man who defied the K.K.K." It did me an immense amount of good, for travelling about in a lawless country for years, prospecting in the mountains, and never carrying a weapon, I found no need for one, but on several occasions should, to all appearances, not have come out alive had I had one, or was not known to be an unarmed man. Nearly all the citizens habitually carried pistols.

By William P. Thompson.

28. THE DISMISSED WORKMAN AS TOLD BY THE HERO OF THE STORY

My business on the railway was usually to work up the notes of the Surveyors, and find where the survey could be improved upon. Sometimes, however, I took charge of a surveying party. On one of these occasions the Chief Engineer, who only visited the line about four times in three years, sent me up a man, with orders to take him on as an employee. The man arrived, with a pair of pistols, and if I remember rightly, a knife, visible as weapons. He looked the picture of a desperado. I enquired what he could do.

"Almost anything."

"Have you done any surveying?"

"No."

"Axework?"

"No."

"Clerking?"

" No."

We put him to work the staff for the leveller. We soon had complaints that the man was spoiling for a fight. Now at that time and in that country, if a man called another a liar or a coward, or gave him warning that after a certain date he would shoot him, it was held equivalent to a challenge to an informal duel, and either of them could shoot the other if the latter was outside a house, and no jury would convict him.

At length my two principal assistants on the corps came to me, and said that unless I interfered, there would be bloodshed in the camp in a day or two. That K—, the new man, was continually flourishing his pistols and trying to get a good excuse to use them. That he also was in the habit of telling disgusting and profane stories round the camp fire, and was demoralising the young men, and further that a number of the corps had banded together and drawn lots, to decide which in turn should warn and shoot him. They further said he is telling one of his disgusting stories at the fire now. I went to the fire and heard him. The following dialogue ensued.

" K—I wish to speak with you."

" Then speak."

" I should have preferred to have spoken to you privately, but seeing you have not the manners to come forward, I must inform you now, that there are numerous complaints of your flourishing your pistols and trying to get up a quarrel, and also of your telling improper stories such as I partly heard, just now, and I must insist on both these practices being at once stopped."

" Or what ? "

" Or you must leave the Corps."

" Mr. T—, during the day-time, I am under your orders and have to obey you ; at night, you (not being a justice of the peace), have absolutely no authority, any more than I have. Further, Colonel L—, the Chief Engineer, took me on, and Colonel L— alone can discharge me."

" That may be true, but if I tell Colonel L—, who will be at the office on Saturday, that either you or I must go, I have a very good idea which he will choose."

The man drew his pistol, cocked it, and pointing it at me said,

" If I have to leave the Corps through your machinations, you shall sup in Hell that night." " Now, boys, when that fellow interrupted me I was just telling you a story, and will now go on with it."

When Colonel L— arrived on Saturday, he was informed of the matter and replied :

"I am delighted to hear it. I thought that man was about the worst ruffian I had seen for some time, and I just sent him up to you to see how long you could stand him; of course he will be discharged to-day without notice."

"That's all very nice for you, Colonel, but the first opportunity he has, after his discharge, he will put a bullet through me."

"Oh, we'll easily arrange that. You take my pistol, and as soon as he has left the room, take a seat by the open window; he has to pass it on his way to the road, and you shoot him dead."

"But that would be sheer murder."

"Not a bit of it. He has given you full warning before witnesses, and after his discharge either can shoot the other, if he be outside the house; everyone will compliment you on it, for he's a notorious ruffian."

I told him I could not do it, and declined his pistol. The men came to be paid, the last one, K—.

"K—, you are discharged without notice. I think you know the reason," said the Colonel.

"I do."

At the same time he looked significantly at me, and tapped his pistol. The moment he was out of the room Col. L— sprang up, shoved a pistol into my hand and said:

"If ever there is murder in a man's face it is in K—'s, and you're a dead man unless you shoot him now!"

I handed him back the pistol and went and sat by the open window. K— walked past with his head about one foot off the window, without ever once looking up. When I had finished my business, the Colonel again offered me the pistol. He said, "K— to a certainty will be hiding on the way to your hotel to shoot you; take the pistol, and walk in the middle of the road and look out."

I declined the pistol, but walked in the middle of the road, till opposite a copse; then walked on the other side, carefully reconnoitring each corner of the fence. Suddenly a man sprang out of the copse and beckoned to me: it was I.H.——the son of the President of the Railroad. He was quite out of breath with running a round-about way through the woods to intercept me. He was a member of our corps.

He said that as he was on his way home he saw a glint of something brilliant through Vandevere's palings, but walked on pretending not to notice it till he got to the next piece of wood. Then cautiously looking back from cover, he saw K—standing with his pistol in his hand intently watching the roadway through a small opening. He had accordingly run his hardest through woods to get round to intercept me in time.

"Now," said he, "I have a splendid Deringer pistol here, take it, it is loaded, and go round Vandevere's house, and you will get within a few feet of K— as you turn the corner, you can then shoot him through the head before he can see you, as he will have his back to you."

I thanked him warmly, but refused his pistol, and felt I must go round the house.

Peeping round the corner, I saw K— with pistol at full cock and his finger on the trigger, standing with his back to me. I watched him a few seconds then noiselessly pulling my shoes off, went on tip-toe up to him, and suddenly putting my hand on his shoulder, said :

"K—, I have twice already had an opportunity of shooting you through the head since you received your pay, but I don't believe in committing murder."

We stared steadily at each other for about a minute, he all the while moving his pistol up and down, then he put it up, and slouching off, saying :

"I thought you were a coward, but I find you are not."

After lunch I went back to the Colonel. He said, "Well, I never expected to see you again, I took it for granted that K— and you would have met, and he would have shot you."

I said, "We *have* met, but it is *he* who has been shot—Quaker fashion."

Having heard the particulars he said :

"You *have* shot him—you need not walk along the centre of the road any more, but I should not have liked to have taken the risk." I told him I had walked on the side walk all the way after encountering him.

That evening there was a knock at my room door.

"Come in." K— walked in.

"Well, K—, what can I do for you ?"

"I have come to ask you to give me a character."

"But what sort of character can I give you ?"

"I've been a month with you, and I am sure I have worked hard, and done my work well."

"Yes you have, and if I give you a character what will you do with it ?" "I intend to go to Major G— (engineer of the competing survey for a rival railway), I hear nearly all his corps is ill, and if you will give me a character I promise solemnly I won't disgrace you."

"Well, I'll trust you."

The written character ran as follows :

"Dear Major G—, The bearer W.K. has been about a month

with us as assistant leveller. During that time he has done his work zealously and well. Beyond this I cannot say anything. He has asked me to give him this introduction to you."

K— read it, opened his mouth to speak three or four times, but seemed too excited to speak. He then said in a broken voice, " I won't disgrace you," and ran off.

Six months after Major G— came to the town where I then was. We naturally met. He said :

" I want to know why you sent K— to me."

" Perhaps I did wrong, but he asked for the letter, how has he got on ? "

" I won't answer a word till I first hear all about him."

I told him all. He then said :

" K— came to me, gave me a military salute and without speaking, handed me your letter. He looked a rough character, but had no weapons that ever I saw. I thought, why has T— sent this man as our work was stopped for want of levellers ? Here we were, doing everything we could to get the better of each other. It cannot be as a spy or murderer : T— has too good a character to do a trick like that. I asked him what wages he had from you, and whether he would take the same from me."

He replied satisfactorily.

" Then I engage you. Take your things to that tent, which you will have to share with two other men."

He saluted, put his things in the tent and sat by the fire till supper-time. It was noticed at supper that he said ' potatoes please,' but no other word. He waited till the other two went to bed, then spread his things down and went to sleep, and since then till three days ago, he has never uttered a word that was not necessary. He never reads, but sits silent by the fire each evening till bed-time. But last Wednesday he came to me and asked if I was going to W—. "

" Yes," I answered.

" Then if you see Mr. T— of the R.R., please tell him how I am getting on."

" He has been a complete enigma to us all—but I now see the reason for his taciturnity. He had promised you he would not disgrace you and knowing he had a foul tongue, he determined not to use it. He has well fulfilled the character you gave him as he has always done his work zealously and. well, has been twice promoted, and is now a leveller at $70 a month.

Soon after this, Green's Corps, was disbanded, and I never heard of K— again.

By WILLIAM P. THOMPSON.

29. QUEEN LYDIA VATEA

The Christian natives (Fiji) were very firm. Two of them meeting near the Mission House shook hands warmly, and, with a cheerful smile, exclaimed, " Heaven is very near ! " They even prepared food to set before their enemies. They retired to the bush—their usual place for prayer—and many a voice was heard there in exulting praise, and many praying for the salvation of their persecutors.

The Heathens said, " O, if you Missionaries would go away ; it is your presence that prevents us killing them. If you would go away, you would not have reached Moturiki," (an island close by) " before all these Viwa people would be in the ovens."

While the consultation was going on in the stone house, Lydia Vatea, the converted Queen, entered, and on her knees, with many tears, besought her kinsman Thakombau (leader of the attacking party) to join the *Lotu* which he threatened to destroy. She told how happy the religion of Jesus made her, and how it fortified her against all fear of death. The great Chief wondered at this strange religion, which enabled its disciples to be so happy in prospect of the ovens.

All that day, the returning warriors, armed with clubs and muskets, were arriving in Viwa, until the place was filled and surrounded . . . the few Christians were powerless. But they showed no wish to resist. They were God's people, and He, in whom they trusted, cared for them. In proportion as the Heathens grew in number, so they seemed to waver in purpose, until they said, " We came to kill these people, and we cannot lift a hand." Towards night they withdrew quietly, acknowledging that the Christians' God was too strong for them. As they passed through the bush to their canoes, many of the converted Viwans, whom they had come to destroy, accompanied them, carrying for them the weapons which had been brought for the expected slaughter.

From the *Life of John Hunt,*
by O. STRINGER ROWE, p. 187.

30. THE DRUNKARD IN THE BOAT

Some years ago a party of youngsters went for a picnic in a Coastguard's motor boat to visit the opposite coast of one of the Irish Loughs. Half-way there the captain brought out a bottle of whiskey, which he proceeded to drink neat, so that on arrival he was unable to stand. On the return journey he pulled out of his locker a second bottle of whiskey and began to help himself, at the same time giving confusing and contradictory orders to his engineer. The eldest of the party was an Irish girl of about 16, who whispered to her English friend, " This can't go on, I must take the tiller and the command of this boat." Her friend answered, " Whatever will happen ? " and the Irish girl replied, " I don't know ". She went up to the Captain and said to him very quietly, " Give me that bottle of whiskey." " What do you want it for," replied he. " I want it for myself," she said, looking him full in the face. He handed her the bottle and she threw it into the sea, saying, " I am in command of this boat now. Give me the tiller." He got up quite quietly and took another seat. The girl brought the party safe to land and next day received the captain's humble apologies. " What can I do for you," said he, " to show how sorry I am ? " to which she answered, " Wear the blue ribbon and keep your pledge." This he faithfully did.

LADY GIBB.

31. WHY ENGLISH POLICE ARE UNARMED

Some years ago, the question of arming the Metropolitan Police and the County Constabulary was seriously considered. As no unanimous decision could be reached by the authorities, the rank and file were asked to express an opinion and, though crime was at that time on the increase they voted against the measure by an overwhelming majority, on the ground that it would provide an additional incentive to violence for the criminal as well as the custodian of the law. When one reflects that the English is one of the very few police forces in the world which is not armed, and that there is less crime in England than in most civilised states, one could hardly wish for a more striking example of the principle that violence begets nothing but reprisal.

From The Friend, March 23rd, 1934.

32. ADELIA FOX AT BEAR'S GAP

" The sending of a missionary into Bear's Gap, Kentucky, was a great factor in the reformation of the State. It was no uncommon thing at the Gap for the people to wake up some morning and find the father of a family lying dead because of the work of someone " in whiskey " as they said.

And into the very heart of this seething whirlpool of wickedness went Adelia Fox, a Sunday School teacher, of Plymouth Congregational Sunday School, Toledo. . . . She held her first meeting at the school-house on a Sunday evening arriving late and finding a crowded house. They had come with pistols and whiskey bottles and promises of how they would run the preacher out on the first visit. But when the slim young girl . . . entered . . . one and all gaped and admired, and gaped again. . . . The Mission board had believed that a strong man was needed to cope with those ruffians, but Adelia Fox, on the evening of her first visit, set all those theories at naught. She had been with them but a few hours, but she had rolled up an army of protectors and friends such as no person in Bear's Gap had ever known. Each man, woman and boy and girl was ready to take up cudgels in her defence. Her innocent sweetness was more of a safeguard than the best rifle she could have bought."

The Girl Missionary of Bear's Gap,

by GRACE BATELER SANDERS.

From the *Son of Temperance,* July, 1916.

33. ESCAPE THROUGH THE BOXER REBELLION

This is the story of the escape of the writer and his wife (who was expecting a baby), their two children aged three and four, and another woman missionary, in the days of the Boxer Rebellion in China. They were absolutely at the mercy of the crowds throughout their journey, and time after time death seemed inevitable. Yet they ultimately arrived at the coast in safety, though neither the poor wife nor her baby long survived its birth.

In order to reach safety they had to travel a thousand miles in sixty-seven days in an exceptionally hot summer.

The following are typical of the many extraordinary escapes which took place all along their route.

One night the party had to spend in a village where the people tried to press in on them in the room where they had taken shelter. The Glovers managed to keep the people out all night by sitting on a bundle of clothing in the window, but in the morning the crowd poured in examining everything. " As they put their sinister faces close to ours, and examined the colour of our eyes, my heart sickened with fear, and I trembled as they drew the children forward and said, " Look at these (little devils) their eyes are as blue as the big ones." A devil is known by its blue eyes in China, and Mr. Glover felt certain that death would follow, especially as two steel stabbers were produced, and the missionaries were ordered to walk in single file along a narrow passage to the street in front of their captors. " Dense masses of people lined the roadway on either side, but our appearance was greeted not . . . by the sudden outcry of a riotous rabble, but by a silence so profound as to be awful to the sense . . . surely this was but the calm before the storm." But to their amazement, and with no explanation, the local Magistrate took their side, accompanying them to the boundary of his town, and retired.

Another time, when the party had had no food for twenty hours, they were surrounded by an armed hostile crowd. One of their faithful Chinese servants told them they must get away, and the crowd silently allowed them to do so. They entered a gully in the hills, and could not but feel forlorn, with no money, no food, no conveyance, 700 miles from safety, and with armed riff-raff before and behind them. They sat awaiting death. At last a Boxer officer appeared and said to the crowds, " What are you doing, letting these foreign devils sit here ? Why don't you kill them ? " The reply was that they were going to beat and strip them first. " No," said the officer. " Kill them outright, that's our first business," but after questioning them, he left. Their servant managed to get bread for the children—it was snatched away, so also was Mrs. Glover's wedding ring, yet even this she did not resist.

At last there was a roar of " Rob " and they were all set on and hurled into the road, amidst the tumult of people. Mr. Glover was stripped of all but his belt and socks, and the children were distracted with terror. The little girl saw a man coming at her with a sword, she prayed to God for safety, and he turned away.

At last, at sunset, a man said to them, " Why do you stay here ? Be off with you." The crowd walked off as if held back and let them go.

So through incident after incident the Glovers refused to show any resistance or resentment, taking everything with calm courage. Even the little boy refused to cry when suffering awful hunger, thirst and sunburn, because he saw it pained his mother.

Imprisonment, illness, alternate hopes and fears, all followed before at long last they were welcomed by native Christians and tended with loving care.

A Thousand Miles of Miracle,
by THE REV. ARCHIBALD GLOVER.

34. PSALMS INSTEAD OF PISTOLS

A policeman jumps between a group of men fighting in one of the streets of Jerusalem. He uses neither force nor threat; all he does is to recite with resounding voice a psalm which states that no quarrel resulting from a conflict of opinions is ever decided through violence. His voice is neither piously exhorting nor hypocritically mild, quite the contrary; it contains a vehement "Don't you know?" an angry surprise: "You foolish fellows, how could you have forgotten this truth?" He holds his psalm up to them, as other policemen elsewhere point to police regulations or threaten with fines. He uses the psalm as an argument, appropriate, pertinent, universally accepted. The fighters stop hitting instantly and continue to fight verbally for a little while, rather ashamed of themselves and more in order to justify themselves than to go on quarrelling, and soon go their separate ways. The policeman is a Jew, the fighting men were poor, simple workmen, Jews and Arabs.

Translated from
Felix Salten, Neue Menschen auf alter Erde.

35. G. F. WATTS-DITCHFIELD AND HIS VISITOR

"Take, for instance, a man, a regular scamp, who was nearly always drunk, and who earned good money, and yet allowed his wife and children to almost starve while the former was scarcely ever without a black eye. This man, try as I would, I never could interview. He was a man with a most violent temper and easily aroused: so one day I called, and left with the woman in the next room a message which, to say the least, was far from complimentary to him, and not over polite, and then I prayed that this might bring him on the Saturday night. Bring him it did, for being admitted he fairly rushed into the room in a frenzy of temper, asking what I meant by leaving such a message for him and threatening what he would do, and shaking his fist meanwhile. A sudden thought struck me, and turning round I locked the door, put the key in my pocket, and calmly sitting down, observed that I always liked a man to finish whatever he took in hand, and that if I had left the door unlocked the other men would have rushed in and stopped him, but that now it would take them five minutes to knock the door down, and so he could proceed. For a moment I thought I was in for it, for his fist came perilously near to my nose, but as he stormed I inwardly lifted up my heart to God and little by little managed here and there to get a word in, and then at last I said, " Well, no man goes out of here until I have prayed with him." He would not kneel down, but stood upright as I prayed. The door was then unlocked and he went. All the next week he was in my thoughts and prayers, and on the next Saturday, he was the first man to walk into my study asking to sign the pledge. Not only has he kept it, but . . . is . . . now " a good husband and father."

Fishers of Men,
by G. F. WATTS-DITCHFIELD.

36. FREDERICK CHARRINGTON PROTECTED BY STREET GIRLS

On one occasion, five young " bloods " arrived at a Music Hall in the East End, and were accosted and remonstrated with, by Frederick Charrington, the earnest temperance advocate. " With faces flushed with drink, their eyes blazing with anger, they advanced on the young evangelist, loudly expressing their determination to " do for him ".

Then occurred, in an instant, one of the most pathetic and dramatic things of which I have ever heard.

Several wretched girls, who had been with these young men . . . turned on their patrons.

They made a ring round Frederick, snarling like tigresses, and using—so Mr. Charrington has told me—the most appalling and awful language it is possible to conceive. They told the young men from the West End that they would tear them in pieces rather than that they should touch a single hair of Mr. Charrington's head.

The Great Acceptance,
by GUY THORNE.

37. MAHSUD HOSPITALITY

Lately I read a paragraph in the *Nation* discussing the bombing of the Mahsud villages in Afghanistan by some British airmen. The incident commented upon by this paper happened when " one of the bombing planes made a forced landing in the middle of a Mahsud village," and when " the airmen emerged unhurt from the wreckage, only to face a committee of five or six old women who happened to escape the bombs, brandishing dangerous-looking knives." The Editor quotes from the London *Times*, which runs thus :

" A delightful damsel took the airmen under her wing and led them to a cave close by, and a ' malik ' (chieftain) took up his position at the entrance—keeping off the crowd of forty who had gathered round, shouting and waving knives. Bombs were still being dropped from the air, so the crowd, envious of the security of the cave, pressed in stiflingly, and the airmen pushed their way out in the teeth of the hostile demonstration. They were fed and were visited by neighbouring ' maliks,' who were most friendly, and by a ' mullah ' priest, who was equally pleasant. Women looked after the feeding arrangements, and supplies from Ladha and Razmak arrived safely. On the evening of the twenty-fourth they were escorted to Ladha, there they arrived at daybreak the next day. The escort disguised their captives as Mahsuds as a precaution against attack. It is significant that the airmen's defenders were first found in the younger generation of both sexes."

According to a Mahsud, hospitality is a quality by which he is known as a man, and therefore he cannot afford to miss his opportunity, even when dealing with someone who can be systematically relentless in enmity. From the practical point of view the Mahsud pays for this very dearly, as we must always pay for that which we hold most valuable. It is the mission of civilisation to set for us the right standard of valuation. The Mahsud may have many faults for which he should be held accountable ; but that which has imparted to him more value to hospitality than to revenge may not be called progress, but is certainly civilisation.

By RABINDRANATH TAGORE, in
Woodbroke International Journal. June, 1930.

38. HOSTILE FRONTIER CLAN'S GRATITUDE

While road-building in the Shaktu Valley, in Waziristan, three labourers belonging to the Kakari section of the Bahlolzai Mahsuds were buried by a landslip. Scouts from the Madamir Kalai, under a British officer, extricated two of them alive, and afterwards, at a tribal gathering which a number of women attended, the Kakari clan decided to abandon further hostilities against the scouts as a token of appreciation of their services in rescuing the tribesmen's fellow clansmen. Since this incident no case of sniping at troops in the area has been reported.

From " *The Times* ", Friday, December 31st, 1937.

39. THE CRIMINAL TURNED FRIEND

James H. Causey, an American business man, was asked to give friendly help to a man who had committed so many crimes that most of his adult life had been spent in Sing Sing prison. Mr. Causey took the man into his own house, and entrusted him not only with his silver and other property, but with his quite young children. Not only did the former criminal never betray this trust, but for seven years until his death remained a faithful friend and servant. From one of the cruellest criminals which this famous prison had ever known, he became one of the gentlest of human beings.

J. H. C.

40. THE PACIFIST AND THE KURDS

Edward Richards, an American Conscientious Objector during the war of 1914-18, founded his actions on a belief " that the picture of personality and character demonstrated by Christ is a true picture of the personality and character of God." Further, " that absolute power and utter love as combined in the character of Jesus Christ, are a fundamental fact, in which the man who is trying to follow Christ can trust. In other words, the man following Christ can rely upon a Divine Power which has power over all things. This Divine Power is fundamentally the power of utter love." The force of love is, in fact, the only power great enough to overcome evil. Edward Richards realised, therefore, that if he were to be as true to his convictions in 1917, as the soldiers were to theirs, he must be willing to be killed, without any question of killing in his turn.

There are two suppositious cases frequently presented to the Pacifist as insoluble by his philosophy, which, as so happened, were both experienced in actuality by Richards, viz., first, to be in a room full of women and children, into which break some wild Turks or Kurds, and secondly, to encounter in a crowded street a drunken or crazy man running amok.

In order to test whether his theoretic pacifism would stand

such experiences as these, with which his unsympathetic friends challenged him, Edward Richards determined to go to the wildest and most dangerous part of the world, which he was told was to be found in West Persia. There, a combination of war, racial antipathies and religious fanaticism produced a most uneasy situation, where massacres were not unknown, and terrible diseases were rampant. Edward Richards was put in charge of the orphans, and the industrial relief in the district of which Uroumiah was the centre. After several months of extensive relief work the situation grew even worse. " The ill-will stirred up by the war, the persecutions, the massacres, the assaulting of women, and the carrying off of girls, had intensified to a terrible degree the age-long hatred between the Syrians and the Armenians on the one hand, and the Kurds, Turks, and Moslems on the other. There were thousands of people who had been driven from their homes, and were refugees." On the withdrawal of the Russian army, open warfare broke out between the rival factions, and after several months the regular Turkish army came to the help of the Moslems, and the Armenians and Syrians to the number of nearly 100,000 people were obliged to flee for refuge far away. Most of the American missionaries stayed in their compound, where many refugees, too, came for shelter. Then the Kurds and Turks entered the city, and the setting for pacifist experiment was soon apparent when Edward Richards was in the room with the women and children of the mission, and one invalid man. Then the actual moment arrived, and the Kurds pounded on the door, making the thin panels bulge. Edward Richards walked to it, undid the small bolt, and said " Come in." Three Kurds, with three rifles, entered, surprised at being admitted, and instead of shooting, they demanded money ; so he led them quickly through the room where were the women and children, to the study where small money was kept in a drawer, the larger relief funds in a safe. Dr. Dodd, the invalid missionary, handed the small change to the Kurds and then left Richards to " entertain " the unwelcome visitors. He shall tell his own story. " While the Kurds were rummaging about the room, I walked over to the safe that had the money in it and tried to open it. Like all Russian safes, it was an iron box with a lid like a trunk, the keyhole being in the top of the lid. Finding the safe was locked, I stood there for a moment, and a horrible sinking feeling began to creep over me as the realisation of the situation came to me. There was nothing to do, however, but play the game, and so I turned back to the Kurds who were on the other side of the little room . . . as I turned, one of them suddenly threw up his rifle, covering me, and speaking in Turkish, demanded the key of the safe. Now I honestly did not have the key, and I looked him in the eye over the sights of the rifle, and told him so. Recognising that I was speaking the truth, he put his gun down and began to rummage round again." Then the thought came to Edward Richards that he must " go the second mile " with the robbers and help them in their search : so he began actually to try to open the safe for them, and putting his finger on the keyholes, suggested (in English) that the Kurd should fire at that place, which he did. At that sound his friends in the next room thought, " Well, there goes Richards—the Christian Pacifist is through." But the lock did not spring, and the safe was not opened. The Kurds were growing impatient, " and suddenly one of them without a moment's notice lost control of his temper, threw up his rifle, and hit me on the shoulder with the butt of it. Then a curious thing happened. I had been honestly sincere in trying to help them to open the safe ; I had joined them in their efforts, and considered myself, for the time being one of them. This sudden blow on the shoulder, therefore, was a real surprise to me, and I remember turning and looking at the man who struck me with an expression which must have said to him, ' What are you hitting me for ? I am doing everything I can to help you.' I spoke no word, but he must have read my look, for he put his gun down, and paid no further attention to me."

At long last, the Kurds all left the house, after taking a coat or two, but passing by and leaving some silver on the sideboard, and having done no personal harm to any of the missionaries.

II

Later on came the second test. Edward Richards writes that he was busy in the yard overseeing the shoeing of a horse. There was the usual crowd at the big gate opening on to the street.

" Suddenly I heard an excited roar go up from near the gate. Leaving the horseshoeing, I ran out to see what was going on, and found a panic-stricken group of Syrians and Armenians peeping into the large mainyard through a narrow little door. From them I learned that a young Armenian, wild-drunk and armed, had rushed into the yards from the street crying that he had come to kill Agha Sader, the wealthy refugee rascal." That is the situation which Edward Richards was called on to face. He argued with himself that if he could approach the drunken man with friendliness and no fear, he might persuade him to go home. He managed to get near to the Armenian before he was seen by him, and this is how he describes what happened. " I smiled and held out my hand, offering to shake hands with him. Here was the test. I strove to appear to this poor drunken mind a friend who was not afraid. He swung round again and caught sight of me, hesitated a moment, and then, drawing himself up to attention, he grounded his rifle, and saluted me in unsteady drunken seriousness. As I came up close to him, I continued to hold out my hand, and much to my surprise, he handed me his gun, saying, as he did so, ' A present '. Taking the rifle in one hand and his arm in the other, I quietly walked with him to the gate." Next day the Armenian came to apologise.

A Test of Faith,
by EDWARD RICHARDS.
Atlantic Monthly, May, 1923.

41. THE KAPP PUTSCH IN BERLIN

Wilfred Wellock was in Berlin at the time of the Kapp Putsch in 1920. It will be remembered that after the German Revolution a number of reactionary generals, among whom was Kapp, retreated to the Baltic with their troops. On Friday, March 12th, however, they organised a coup with the intention of gaining the mastery of the country. The Government, taken unawares, fled to Stuttgart, whilst the invaders proclaimed that a better Government was installed. Their troops numbering about 5,000 occupied all the key positions and were stationed outside all the railway stations, banks, post offices, etc. Consternation reigned, but by the following evening the Independent Socialists had decided on, and organised, action. Although they probably had enough rifles to overcome the usurpers, wiser counsels prevailed, and a general strike was called for Sunday night. It was emphatically ordered, however, that this must be conducted with good humour ; there was to be no provocation, while all Socialists were to fraternise with the soldiers, explain the situation to them, and treat them with the utmost friendliness. By Sunday noon the Socialists were hanging on to the soldiers like flies. The streets were crowded with people. To meet the new danger the Putsch officers sent out all their cavalry to drive the Socialists off their men. But without success. No sooner were the Socialists driven off one set of men than they fixed themselves on to another set.

On the Monday morning the general strike was in full swing and appeared to be 100 per cent. effective. Not a single service, except that of food supply, was running. All traffic, rail and vehicular—was at a complete standstill. Even gas and electricity were cut off. Only cold meals could be secured, while at night the city was in complete darkness. The invaders were completely held up.

This state of affairs continued until Wednesday, by which time the leaders of the Putsch had to acknowledge defeat. They were helpless and had to come to terms which were speedily arranged. It was agreed that the Baltic troops should leave the city at 6.30 on the Thursday evening. At the hour fixed for the departure I stood in Leipzigerstrasse, at the foot of Wilhelmstrasse, and dead on 6.30 the troops appeared. A great concourse of people had assembled to witness the retreat. Yet they were silent. Not a voice could be heard, not a whisper, nothing but the dull tramp of the troops, as they marched, fully accoutred, through the vast crowds of unarmed Berlin citizens who had defeated them with folded arms and good humour and without the firing of a single shot.

Condensed from account by Wilfred Wellock.

42. SAFETY WITHOUT GUN-BOATS

Following her disarmament by the Allies after the First European War, Germany had no gun-boats to send to China wherewith to " protect " her nationals. During the Chinese revolution, when the other Europeans and the Americans were hiding or escaping, the Germans were safe and able to carry on their lives, and their business, as usual, because the Chinese were not terrified by any gun-boats.

43. THE KNIGHTS OF PEACE

At the time of the French occupation of the Ruhr in 1923, the situation between French and Germans was extremely tense there. The latter, unable to rid themselves of their unwelcome visitors, ignored them as far as possible, treating them like ghosts whom they could not see—a very effective way of passively resisting their presence. But one French Protestant Lieutenant, Etienne Bach, made intimate friends with the young Germans in several of the Ruhr towns, and the atmosphere changed in consequence. Bach tells how on Good Friday, " I was in Datteln on the Lippe. The chaplain of our division was a long way away, so

I looked for a church which I could attend. There was none to be found, but in a neighbouring workmen's quarter, I was shown a " Luther-house " where services were held. On entering, my presence disturbed a little those present, but when they heard me singing the hymns heartily, they told each other I was an Alsatian, and that calmed them. Then there came the moment of Holy Communion. What should I do ? Should I draw back out of fear not to cause a sensation ? Why ? It was Jesus and not the worshippers who invited me to His table. And I decided to go up. I let the ones in front go up first, and then, as there were only three more people left I also stepped forward. To my great astonishment I saw I was next to Mr. Wille, the Mayor of Datteln, with whom the military authorities had had the greatest difficulties. I cannot describe the emotion I felt. As we broke the same bread and drank out of the same cup, the clergyman's hand trembled. At this moment I felt what the Holy Communion can be. How marvellous ! These two people, enemies in the eyes of the world, oppressed by the burden of their sins, kneeling side by side before the face of God ! "

After this, many were the difficulties that disappeared, and Bach's good work became known to the authorities who entrusted him with keeping order in one of the towns threatened with communist riots, and there again he won the hearts of the people, and was often invited to speak on French Protestantism, in German meetings. Finally, the French commander-in-chief made enquiries about his success, and wrote, " In my opinion there is no better means of gaining respect for France than to live as good Christians among her foes."

When Etienne Bach returned to France he organised the movement for friendship which had grown up round his work into a union called " Knights of Peace " which has branches in several countries. The " Knights " are bound by the simplest rules, but their lives are based on prayer and a belief in the power of Christ to bring peace to the world.

44. REVOLT AMONG THE SHARE-CROPPERS

" Share-cropper " is the term applied in U.S.A. to a man who owns scarcely anything but his own and his family's labour with which they farm a few acres of cotton belonging to a planter, who provides a house, tools and seed, and pays the tenant half the price of the cotton produced. They are amongst the poorest and the most oppressed people to be found in so-called civilised countries.

To attempt to remedy their grievances a few of the share-croppers decided in 1934 to form a Trades Union, with white and negro members. This roused the anger of the planters, and the most brutal and unfair methods were used against them, although it was legally constituted. Families were evicted for union-membership, meetings were broken up, men were kicked, ill-treated and put into prison on trumped up charges, and violence and starvation made a veritable reign of terror in Arkansas, resulting in many deaths.

During these days " the men who directed the activities of the union lived in the expectation of immediate death. Without sleep, without food, and often without hope—but never without faith in the ultimate triumph of their cause—they directed a brilliant struggle along the lines of non-violent resistance which won for them the support of the whole country. Had it not been, said a *New York Times* reporter who visited the scene, for the policy of passive resistance which was adopted by the leaders of the union, Arkansas would have been visited by a terrible massacre.

" The back of the terror was broken not by resorting to the violent tactics of the defenders of the system but by the written word and the ceaseless activity of the thousands of disinherited men, women and children who lived for the union, but were ready to die that the union might live and bring some measure of peace, freedom and security to their children."

From *Revolt among the Share-croppers,*

by HOWARD KESTER. New York.

45. HOW TO TREAT BURGLARS

As a rule, I am alone in the house, except for the domestics who sleep on an upper landing, but on a certain night my daughter-in-law, C., occupied the guest room. In the middle of the night I heard footsteps along the passage outside my bedroom door and the door of my library adjoining, and, thinking that C. might be unwell, I hastily rose, opened the door, turned on the passage light, and to my horror . . . I found myself face to face with two ruffianly looking men.

Now I always had a horror of the thought of burglars, since an unpleasant experience in my father's house, but strangely enough . . . intuition . . . came to my rescue. For without a moment's thought, although my heart was beating furiously, I quietly placed my hand on the arm of the man who was close to me and on the point of escaping, and I said in a friendly way : " Hullo ! what are you doing here ? " " We are burglars," replied the man. " Yes, I can see you are," said I, as I glanced at the floor, which was strewn with my papers and belongings, and at his pockets, which were bulging with my property. " But," I continued, as I looked into his eyes, and felt that at the back of all this unpromising exterior here was a fellow human soul, who had just gone astray, " isn't that rather a poor game to play ? Come, let us sit down and have a talk about it, and find out why you are burgling. I expect you have been up against hard times." " Yes," said the man, " but we didn't expect this." " No," said I, cheerily, " and I didn't expect you." Then I saw that the second man had hidden himself, and was crouching behind a screen near the door, so I turned to him and said : " Come along, you, and sit down and let's have a talk." He stood up, and I saw that he held in his hand something bright and shining. I thought it was a pistol, so I asked : " What have you in your hand ? " (I still had my hand on the arm of the other man, who was close to and facing the door.) He said it was a torch. " Oh yes," said I, reassured, " well, come on then, don't be afraid, I am not going to hurt you." But he was a coward, and brushing roughly past me, nearly knocking me over, he rushed past me down the two steps to the landing, and down the staircase. I ran after him to call him back. " Hi ! you—come along back," I called, " you are not going to leave your mate all alone with me ? " (as though it would be dangerous for the mate) and like a lamb the man came upstairs again, and I made them both sit down in the library, whilst I talked to them, quietly and suggestively, taking the line that they had probably drifted into this kind of life through unfortunate circumstances, and that unless they called a halt they would probably go on from bad to worse, and end by committing a bad crime, with its inevitable consequences.

By this time C., who had heard us skirmishing on the stairs, joined us, and though slightly surprised at the sight which greeted her, took the cue and sat silently enjoying the situation. Then suddenly I said : " Oh ! perhaps you are hungry—let us go down and get something to eat," so I led a little procession down to the kitchen, the three following closely behind. A queer picture, for as a matter of fact I was wearing an old garden coat over my pyjamas, having lent my dressing-gown to C., and I was certainly not looking my best. . . . .

Arrived at the kitchen, I went to the larder and to my disappointment found that there was no cold meat. So I apologised to my guests, who were now seated at the kitchen table, saying I was awfully sorry that there was no meat, but I would fetch some eggs. Now the eggs were in a basket at the other end of the house, and the burglars could well have taken the opportunity to escape had they mistrusted me and suspected that I had perhaps gone to telephone the police, but they sat tight, whilst C. prepared the saucepan for the eggs, with which I returned and made some tea for us all. I discovered afterwards that they had previously helped themselves to whisky in the dining-room, and were not in need of sustenance. I commented on their poor appetites and they said : " What could you expect ? It has been rather an exciting evening for us."

Now, when we were upstairs I had made them give up the spoils with which their pockets were filled, and they told me that they had surrendered everything, but noticing on the floor (near an iron box, in which I keep papers, under my desk) that a case that had contained the miniatures of my War medals was empty, I asked for the medals. " Where are they ? " " Dunno." " Then please find them, you must know where they are. They are of no real value to you, but of great sentimental value to me. Where are they ? " " P'raps they are downstairs." " Well, one of you go down and find them." One of them meekly went off, was gone rather a long time, and I learned afterwards that he had fetched the medals from a suitcase which they had filled with silver articles, etc., and had hidden in the shrubs in the garden. That suitcase they had taken from my library, and I grieve to say they had destroyed the papers therein contained (including some of the records of my life). But the man gave back the medals.

The men were, obviously, not hungry, and as conversation was all on my side I brought the evening party to a close by saying it was time for them to go, as I was sleepy and wanted to get back to bed. I showed them to the front door, saying : " You didn't come in at the front door (they had broken in through a window in the south veranda), " but you shall go out by it." I gave them ten shillings each in case they were hard up. " How are you going home ? If by Tube you had better have some small change," so I gave them each another shilling, shook hands with them and they departed, generously leaving the suitcase full of my belongings in the garden for me to find the next day. . . .

After the men had gone I discovered that a case that had contained my husband's War medals, in the iron box, was empty, and, of course, I feared that I should never recover the medals. But that evening by the last post I received a registered packet. This contained my husband's medals and a letter from the burglars, unsigned of course—saying they were sorry they had taken the medals by mistake, and thanking me for my hospitality.

A fortnight after the episode just described, as I came down to breakfast, I was met by the manservant who said: "Madam, I am sorry to tell you, we have had burglars again." This time they took all the things they had returned before, including some precious trophies won by my sons.

I don't believe the same men were concerned, but they probably belonged to a gang, and when they recorded their experience and came back empty-handed it was probably decided that the job must be carried out. . . . I had told the original burglars that I would not give them away to the police, because I had hoped to have been able to rescue them from their present life. So when in duty bound I informed the police that I had been burgled, and they asked me for a description of the men I kept my promise.

I said to the Inspector, who came to see me, I supposed he would think I was a fool for behaving as I did, but to my surprise he said: "No," he thought that under the circumstances I had probably saved my life, or at least saved myself from injury through being knocked down, etc., etc.

From *Miracles and Adventures*,
by MRS. ST. CLARE STOBART, p. 25.
(Rider, 1935).

46. ROTARIANS IN PAIRS

During a state of inter-racial and inter-religious rioting in a large Indian city, the local Rotary Club decided to try the influence of Rotary fellowship. In pairs the Rotarians of opposing races and religions walked through the streets arm-in-arm to the amazement of the rioters of both factions, and shortly peace came to the city.

It was not done by adopting resolutions or by mobilising the Rotary Club and making a military force of it; it was done by Rotarians letting it be observed that they were friends.

From *The Manchester Guardian*.

It is well known that the frontier tribes on the north-west border of India, frequently raid their neighbours, and commit aggressive actions. This force is met by the Government with more force.

Theodore Pennell, a medical Missionary, who came out to the frontier in 1892, was a man whose whole life proclaimed that he followed the teaching of the Prince of Peace, of Him who when He was reviled, reviled not again, and this was so new to the lifelong habits of the warriors of the Border that at first they felt there must be some ulterior motive behind it. But though they met his first advances with suspicion, and even with unkindness, and persecution, Dr. Pennell continued to minister to their bodily needs, relieving their suffering, healing their sicknesses, easing their minds of burdens, making their sorrows his own; he lived among them as one of themselves, wearing their dress; speaking their language, doing his best to understand them; he was never too tired to go to a sick bed, he demanded nothing in return for his services. It was impossible for the generous-hearted Pathan to resist such a man. His bravery made a special appeal to them, for he travelled all over their country, unafraid, and unarmed. Dr. Pennell knew that Mullahs preached that his death was a duty enjoined on the faithful follower of the Prophet because he was by his life and teaching demonstrating the beauty of the teaching of Christ, and thus perhaps winning people to another allegiance. Yet this fearless man went alone and unarmed as always, to visit such a Mullah in his own home, when he heard that the Mullah had sent out a band of young men to find this " Bannu Daktar Sahib ", and bring him back alive or dead.

Dr. Pennell's arrival at the Mullah's village just after this edict had sent forth a number of fiery hotheads, who had sworn to take his life, naturally embarrassed the Mullah, who had never met the young Englishman before, and had no idea of the kind of man he was. To see a man whose life was in such jeopardy standing before him, with simple unconcern, though he bore no arms, was almost impossible for the Mullah to believe, as was Dr. Pennell's quiet explanation of his visit, his saying he had just heard of the Mullah's order to his followers, and had taken the first opportunity after his day's work in his Hospital was finished to ride the thirty odd miles to see the Mullah, and ask him why he had issued this order. The Mullah's surprise at the Doctor's fearlessness was merged in his respect for him, and being a Pathan, and therefore hospitable by nature as well as by religion, he allowed his admiration for the young Englishman's intrepid behaviour to add weight to his own instinct, and he ordered his men to provide a meal for the guest. Once he broke bread with Dr. Pennell he was bound by his tribal laws, as well as his Moslem idea of the obligations of a host, to protect his guest. So when his hot-headed " jawans " heard the news that the Mullah had eaten with the very man he had asked them to bring in alive or dead, they were unable to understand the situation. Meanwhile, Dr. Pennell had a long talk with the Mullah, and won his heart, for he could not but see that the people of the whole countryside were benefiting enormously by the skill and loving service of this man. Dr. Pennell had a wonderful way of discovering the points of contact between himself and people of apparently widely diverse views, and the Mullah was soon regretting his action in despatching the young warriors of the tribe on their mission of hate.

After their talk, Dr. Pennell said he was very tired, and as he must be on his way back before dawn the next day, he asked to be allowed to retire. In the hot weather in India everyone sleeps out of doors. The ordinary string-bed of the country is used by guests and hosts alike, and for safety, over the border, as well as on both sides of it, the sleepers congregate in one place. The Mullah's bed was in the centre of the row ; he put one for his guest between his own and his son's. Very soon after his head had touched the primitive pillow made by the puggri, Dr. Pennell was fast asleep. When the baulked and disappointed warriors returned they were astounded to see their quarry lying peacefully asleep.

" Now is our chance to kill him," said one.

" He is my guest," protested the Mullah.

" But not ours," argued the men.

" Well, look at him, he is alone and unarmed among declared enemies, and yet he sleeps with absolute calm. Could we kill a man of such courage ? . . . " The Pathan youths had no more to say, they respected courage too, and so as on other occasions when he was at the mercy of raiders, and had taken no precautions for his own safety, his life was saved because he trusted their own good sense, as well as having a faith that was equal to such demands.

Dr. Pennell was once invited by a freebooter Chief, Chikki, to come to his fortress across the Border to doctor some of his people. There was a price on Chikki's head, and he could not enter either British or Afghan territory, nor indeed could any of the two thousand outlaws who formed his " army ". Two of the outlaw's own friends came as escort to take Dr. Pennell to his place. Dr. Pennell refused a British escort as they would scarcely have been safe. He was as usual unarmed, and he went alone. The fortress was on a height, and a difficult path led to it. Every battlement and tower was bristling with armed men.

When Chikki asked the doctor to come and argue with his Mullah, he sat himself between the two of them, and said to his guest, " Now Doctor Sahib, you and the Mullah can discuss your respective teachings, while I sit between you with my rifle across my knees. Don't let the sight of these armed rascals of mine all round worry you, if any one of them should trouble you, I will put a bullet into him at once."

The result of Dr. Pennell's visit to Chikki was that the Outlaw became his friend, and when a Frontier war broke out shortly after, Chikki sent in a message to him to say that he was keeping 8,000 men out of the fight, because of his friendship with the English doctor Sahib of Bannu. The withdrawal of 8,000 picked men meant a great handicap to the fighting forces of the tribes, and the " War " was soon over, and peace restored.

It was for incidents such as this that a famous Commander-in-Chief is reported to have said that, " *Pennell was worth two regiments on the Frontier.*"

MRS. PENNELL.

48. THE PACIFICATION OF LIBERIA

In 1932 the Government of Liberia, in West Africa, appealed to the League of Nations for help in subduing turmoil amongst its tribes. Houses were being burnt, crops being destroyed, and many people had been killed. The League Council appointed Dr. Melville Mackenzie, a member of their Secretariat, who had formerly helped the Friends' Relief Committee in the famine days in Russia, to go to Liberia. He was joined by a representative of the Liberian Government for whom they acted as representatives.

Dr. Mackenzie saw that the root of the trouble was the possession of arms, which resulted in fear of each other. He managed to persuade the chiefs and their tribes that their quarrels could only be really settled by marking out the boundaries, which should be done as soon as they stopped fighting and gave up their arms. He succeeded in achieving this in two months, and when the fighting ceased, the boundaries were fixed, a town was rebuilt by the tribe who destroyed it, and settlement of their quarrel was peaceably effected.

From *Peace-making in Africa.*
Friends' Peace Committee.

49. " TEACHING THE BLACKS A LESSON "

In Northern Austrialia, some Japanese and a British Policeman were murdered by the Natives. There was the usual cry for a punitive expedition to " teach the Blacks a lesson." But the Australian Government was so wise as to send, instead, a group of unarmed Missionaries. At first there was suspicion, then they won their way ; they were invited to stay, were given houses and finally were appointed judges of the suspected murderers.

50. PUPILS AND PIRATES

Hong-Kong, *February* 2.

Providentially children seldom number piracy among their experiences even in Eastern waters. It must be unique to be in charge of a shipload of European boys and girls captured by pirates and delivered unscathed after nearly three days in their hands. Seated now at the very table at which the pirates were sitting only yesterday and writing with a pen which two frenzied pirates had been too blind with excitement to take from my breast pocket, I have written a first-hand account of what took place and of the feelings we experienced throughout the episode.

Seventy children of the China Inland Mission's School at Chefoo embarked at Shanghai under my care and that of four lady teachers on January 29 after their usual winter holiday. That afternoon, nine hours from Shanghai and within sight of one of the best-known lighthouses on the coast, we were pirated, while many of the boys and girls were still about upon the deck. At the first sign of a scuffle with the guards, before I realised the full gravity of the situation, I sent them inside, but almost at once I was attacked by a couple of pirates. One brandished a small pistol and the other prodded me vigorously with a wooden holster as if in search of arms. He was too wild to see the notes which I took out for him and soon went on, as his companion had already done. We were all rounded up into the saloon, and before long four frantic pirates were confronting a crowded room full of Europeans who seemed to be as calm as their captors were excited.

Captors and Captured

A few children gave way to alarm, but on the whole we seem to have been possessed by a quiet fearlessness, which was in marked contrast to the imminent danger of stray shots from the brandished weapons of the pirates. During a critical parley of two hours not one of the loaded pistols went off in the crowded room, though only one had its safety catch on. The children remained quiet. Some went off to sleep.

Gradually the pirates' excitement subsided to something nearer the self-possession of their prisoners. The leader of the gang was a hardened young man with seven piracies to his record, who has been a leader for seven out of the thirteen years which have passed since, as a lad, he started piracy. He immediately and almost smilingly assented to every request to allow the children to have their supper and go quietly to bed. We saw a little of what was meant by the Master Himself when He said : " Thou couldest have no power at all against me, except it were given thee from above."

The four ladies and the forty children with them in the cabins off the saloon lived in the constant presence of three or four armed pirates, yet for three days they showed great fortitude, and kept the children quiet and steady in cramped conditions.

Yesterday afternoon, the third day, we successfully sneaked across the usual track of coastal vessels and made for a point which the pirates knew. A vain attempt was made to catch two junks in which to set the pirates ashore and the ship went close in to land and circled to try to catch the more nimble junks which worked in with wind and current to the shore. At last we captured a junk, into which the pirates began to load their booty.

The Tables Turned

Suddenly an aeroplane appeared, and the men, who had been about to leave in perfect quiet and friendliness, were panic-stricken. The three chief men cut the rope and fled down-wind in the junk, leaving about six of their companions stranded in the ship. We were all unarmed, and the situation was critical, but though the controlling hand of the leader was gone they waited for a boat to be lowered and went off in it.

When they were clear of the ship word was given that we were free, and the girls and boys came out to enjoy a new freedom outside. A second aeroplane arrived, circled round the ship several times, and then flew off to make her report and to send a destroyer to meet us. The last pirates had taken as temporary hostages one officer and the Chinese wireless operator, who had acted most efficiently as interpreter ever since our capture. These and the boat's crew were left on the shore while the pirates fled off inland. When at last the former were back on board, full speed was made for Hong-Kong, and we soon met a destroyer which escorted us in.

The manner of the pirates was in some ways paradoxical. They were fierce and pitiless on the one had, yet kindly and considerate to the children on the other. One of their great pleasures was to call for a basket of oranges and to dole them out to the children. They repeatedly said they did not want passengers' effects, yet they investigated the ladies' cabins and also relieved even the children of all their pocket money except small change. They allowed us regular and perfectly sufficient meals, yet made those of the ladies and girls a most trying ordeal by the proximity of their weapons. The pirates had aimed at seizing $250,000 in notes from the cargo, yet on being disappointed of that they were quite friendly and cheerful and contented themselves with a few hundreds in cash.

> By Mr. F. N. Duncan of the China Inland Mission
> School, Chefoo, who was in charge of the children.
> From " The Times," February 23rd, 1935.

51. A SAFE DRIVE IN THE BALKANS

After the First World War a group of American Friends were engaged in reconstruction work at Pec, in Yugo-Slavia, fifty miles from the nearest railway station at Mitrovitza. This journey was across wild country, the haunt of brigands called Comitadji. When I visited these workers, I found that the long drive was made in native carts, called Kolas, and the usual fire-arms were dispensed with, in accordance with our Quaker principles. Not only so, but as I set out, I found that the mail-bag was entrusted to my driver, and that other Kolas were accompanying us, for the para-doxical safety of lack of arms. These journeys were always made in safety.   A. R. F.

52. THEY KEPT THEIR HEADS

As our boat crept along the river toward Chengtu, China, we became conscious that the boatmen were rowing in dead silence instead of chanting their songs; that the captain was peering anxiously into the thickets alongshore; that even the little river docks, normally so lively, were almost deserted. We asked what it meant, and finally the captain admitted the truth: "Bandits have been killing and robbing in this district. They know you are on board and have been following for hours along the shore. And we must tie up at the next pier."

Miss Miller and I, two white women, would be a choice prize; half-sick with apprehension we saw the pier just ahead. As we made fast, the boatmen adjusted their long knives, and the captain brought out a shotgun; not a soul stirred in the village. I heard a low cry from one of the boatmen: the bandits were coming, three of them.

"Captain! Put the gangplank down—I'm going ashore!" Miss Miller suddenly cried. He started to expostulate, but she jumped to the dock and, as the bandits approached, bowed low. The leader, a great burly fellow, looked puzzled, then returned her bow. "Thank you, gentlemen," she said, smiling. "Thank you for coming!" The outlaws looked at her, bewildered. "We had heard there were bandits in this country," Miss Miller went on, "and we have been very frightened. Now we know we are safe, and we thank you for coming to protect us."

The leader turned to his companions with a wide grin; they grinned also, and nodded. "We are gentlemen, as you have said," he replied. "There is nothing to fear. We will stand guard and you will be safe."

All night those three, and five or six others, squatted beside the boat with their guns across their knees. And in the morning we went on our way, leaving them bowing and grinning on the pier.

Dr. Agnes Edmonds, former head of Gamble
Memorial Hospital, Chungking, China, quoted
by Lowell Thomas in The Commentator.

53. RAIDERS INTO CONSTABLES

Sir Hubert Murray was for more than twenty years the Governor of Papua. When he went there, raids were a common occurrence. When they happened, he walked out to the village which had been attacked, with his followers, and asked who were the guilty people. If he could obtain no facts, he walked out into the wild country often being nearly shot by arrows, which were probably poisoned. His answer was to put down attractive presents, which were soon seized, and negotiations became easy. When the guilty were given up, he did not punish them, except by telling them not to raid, but instead made them come with him on his walks of investigation. After three years of such instruction in his methods of justice, the former raiders were sent back, proudly arrayed as village constables in blue uniforms.

From *The Manchester Guardian,* June 16, 1936.

Further, it is stated in the official review of the administration in Papua, written by Sir H. Murray, that " the work of pacification is commonly carried out without bloodshed even among the fiercest tribes. . . . In Papua the ' punitive expedition ' with its swift injustice does not exist. If a man is murdered, we arrest the murderer . . . we do not punish (his) village."

54. A BRAVE BISHOP

The Rt. Rev. A. H. Anstey, Anglican Bishop of Trinidad—the Caribbean oil, pitch, sugar and cocoa metropolis—was one of the outstanding heroes of the recent general strike in that British Colony. With marines on their way from the British warship *Exeter,* volunteers being hastily mobilised after rioting in which a police corporal was burned alive, an officer killed and others wounded, the brave Bishop armed with nothing but a smile walked into a mob of strikers in the island's southern capital of San Fernando and converted an angry mob into a friendly crowd.

Bishop Anstey's smile is the biggest I have ever met and a photograph of the actual scene, which I have before me as I write, shows the Bishop in action surrounded by a smiling crowd of negroes and East Indian sugar-cane cutters. The negro size grin is well-known ; but Bishop Anstey can out-grin them. When someone audaciously knocked off his hat, he smiled even more widely. " It enabled more people to recognise me," he said afterwards.

From *The World Observer,* September, 1937.

55. FOREST FRIENDSHIP

From time to time, news leaks through to the outer world of primitive conditions in unsurveyed forests, which remind us of the long way man has come on his march to civilisation. Thus, I am grateful to an old fellow traveller, C. W. Domville Fife, for recording the measures which were taken by Brazil's Indian Protective Service in establishing friendly relations with savages in the hinterland wilderness of the deep Amazon country. They can be found in his recent book, *Modern South America*.

" Attraction posts " were established in the jungle and stocked with objects likely to interest the savage. Presents were hung on trees, music was played to them and night after night an interpreter stationed in a crow's nest would cry out a message of amity and goodwill.

" Often at first," says Mr. Domville Fife, " the only reply was the zip ! zip ! of darts and javelins hurled into the branches." But gradually the inoculation " took " and in time savage distrust was overcome.

From *The World Observer*.

56. THE PEACEFUL STRIKE IN MONTANA

Butte, Montana, U.S.A. had frequently been the scene of bloody labour strikes, but in 1934 a strike of four and a half months against a Copper Mining Company, which had been all-powerful for years, passed without any violence, thanks to the action of the Governor. The Sheriff gave assurances that picketing would be allowed if peacefully carried out, and although the Company imported armed gunmen, the crowds dispersed without any casualties, when appealed to by the Police and the union officials. The Governor discussed the whole matter with the strikers, and the picketing by the latter was in order to prevent the Company from instigating further violence. As a result there were no more street fights, and after four and a half months the Company and the men conferred together and a higher minimum wage than before was guaranteed. The strike cost nothing for special police work, nor was there any loss of life or property.

The Christian Century, Chicago, October 17, 1934.

57. THE PACIFIST AND THE RUSSIAN SOLDIERS

After the Russian Revolution, a Russian Pacifist was living in a village in the Ukraine with his mother and sister and her boy, when one night five " Red " soldiers demanded to come in to search the house for weapons. He made no difficulty, and finding they were tired and hungry he put food before them. When they left they told him that they had intended to kill them.

There was a Colonel living at the other end of the village who barricaded his door against them. They burst it in and killed them all.

One of the leading peasants said to the Pacifist next day, " You did miss an opportunity. You might have poisoned the meat, and then they would all have been dead in the morning." And he answered, " What would have been the result of that ? The whole village would have been burnt from end to end."

As told by the man himself. August, 1938.

58. THE LEPER DOCTOR IN CHINA

About a year ago a doctor who is giving his life to China went to make a study of an island to see if it would do for a leper colony where he could carry on, without danger of spreading contagion, the marvellous modern medical treatment of leprosy. On the way out he passed the perilous haunt of bandits in safety because a fog hid his boat. But on the way back the bandits spied them and boarded their boat. Here they were at the mercy of brigands who were supposed to have no conscience, no heart, no sympathy, supposed to be actuated only by greed and to know only one force, the guns of their pursuers. This doctor showed them that he had no guns, no weapons of any kind. He told them that he purposely came without defence. He also laid before them his plan of work for the lepers, his desire to save these poor creatures from their sufferings, and his hope to make human love build a better world. With a kind of awe they listened and then left the boat to go on its way in peace, and rowed back to their retreat. Once more the positive way of life, the way of faith, of fearlessness and love had overcome.

The New Quest,
by Rufus M. Jones.
(Macmillan, 1928).

59. THE MISSIONARY'S WIFE IN CHINA

The following true story from "*The Exile*", by PEARL BUCK, is reprinted by kind permission of the author and her publishers, Messrs. Methuen.

Day after day through the Spring no rain fell, and the farmers, waiting for the floods of the rainy season to fill their rice fields, saw their young crops dry up before their eyes. . . .

Carie (the missionary's wife) with her sharp perceptions ever sensitive to changes in the moods of people, felt such a change in the temper of the people of the Chinese city. Few came to Andrew's (the missionary's) little chapel. . . . One Sunday there was not one person. The next day Wang Amah the faithful Chinese servant came back from her marketing and said to Carie, "It is better for us not to go out now on the street." When pressed she added unwillingly, "The people say the gods are angry because foreigners have come into the city. There has never been a drought like this before, and this is the first year there have been foreigners in the city to live. The gods are angry, therefore, they say."

One hot August day (when Andrew was away from home) Carie heard a whisper of voices beneath the open window. . . .

"To-night at midnight we will force the gates and kill them and throw their bodies before the gods so that rain may come."

She rose quickly and went to find Wang Amah. "Go out and listen about the streets," she said. "Find out what you can what is being planned for this night."

Wang Amah went out. In a little while she came back, her eyes staring. She shut all the doors carefully. "Oh, my mistress," she panted, "they are coming to kill you to-night—you and the children. Every white person is to be killed."

That night she put the children to bed early and then sat quietly sewing. . . . The murmur of the city drummed through the stifling, dusty air. She listened to it, striving tensely to catch a change in its tempo. About midnight the change came. The murmur rose and seemed to eddy about the walls of the house. The hour was coming. She rose and called softly to Wang Amah who sat silent in the shadow of the court. "Wang Amah, please prepare the tea now."

Then she went downstairs and set out cups and plates upon the oval table and placed cakes on plates. Then when all was ready as though for a feast she swept and made the room spotlessly neat and set the chairs as for guests. Then she went to the court and to the front gate and threw it wide open.

On the threshold stood a vanguard of men, their faces invisible in the darkness of the hot night. They drew back into the blackness but she did not seem to see them, nor did she falter. She went back to the house and left the door open into the court, turned the oil-lamp high, so that the light streamed outside, and then went upstairs and roused the three children and dressed them and brought them downstairs. They were astonished and silent with the strangeness of the proceeding, but she talked to them naturally, sang a little song to them, and set them on the matting of the floor and gave them their Sunday toys to play with and they fell to playing happily. Then she took up her sewing again and sat down. Wang Amah had brought in pots of tea, and she stood behind the children, motionless, her face expressionless.

All about the house the murmur increased until it was a roar of many voices. When the voices became articulate and very near, Carie rose casually and went to the door and called out, " Will you come in, please ? "

They were already in the court then and at the sound of her voice they swelled forward, a mass of sullen, angry men of the lower working class, in their hands sticks and clubs and knives. She called again kindly, her voice made bright by sheer will, " Come in, friends, neighbours , I have tea prepared."

The men paused at this uncertainly. A few pressed forward. Carie poured the tea out and came forward bearing a cup in both her hands as the polite custom was. She presented it to the tall, surly, half-naked man who seemed to be the leader. His mouth gaped in amazement but he took the cup helplessly. Carie smiled her most brilliant smile upon the faces that gleamed in the light from the wide-flung door.

" Will you come in and drink tea for yourselves ? " she said. " And sit down also. I am sorry my humble house had not enough seats, but you are welcome to what I have." Then she stepped back to the table and pretended to busy herself there. The children stopped playing, and Edwin ran to her side. But she reassured them, gently, " Nothing to be afraid of, darlings. Just some people come to see what we look like—such funny people, who want to see what Americans look like ! They haven't seen Americans before."

The crowd began to edge into the room, staring, gaping, momentarily diverted. Some one whispered, " Strange, she is not afraid ! "

Carie caught the whisper. " Why should I fear my neighbours ? " she asked in well simulated surprise.

Others began to examine the furniture, the curtains, the organ. One touched a note, and Carie showed him how to make the sound come. Then she slipped into the seat and began to play softly and to sing, in Chinese, " Jesus, Thy Name I Love."

Dead silence filled the room until she finished. At last the men looked at each other hesitatingly. One muttered, " There is nothing here—only this woman and these children—— "

" I go home," said another simply, and went out.

Others, still sullen, lingered, and the leader halted to look at the children. He held out his hand to Arthur and the rosy, friendly little boy, having seen brown faces about him all his life, smiled and seized the man's lean dark forefinger. The man laughed delightedly and cried out, " Here's a good one to play."

The crowd gathered about the children then, watched them, began to grow voluble in their comments, picked up the American toys to examine and play with them. Carie, watching, was in an agony of fear lest a rough movement might frighten one of the children and so change the temper of the men. . . . At last the leader rose and announced loudly, " There is nothing more to do here, I go home."

It was the signal to follow. One by one, with backward stares, they passed into the court and into the street. Carie sat down again, suddenly faint, and taking the baby into her lap rocked him gently. The men, lingering at the threshold of the gate, looked last upon her thus. . . . She went down and closed the gate. . . . A wind had risen out of the south-east, a wind like the herald of a typhoon. . . . it was fresh and cool with the coolness of the distant sea. . . . She lay sleepless for a long hour and fell at last into a light sleep, and later awoke. Upon the tile roof above her was the music of rain pouring down, streaming from the corners of the house, splashing upon the stones of the court. . . .

60. SLEEPING BEAUTY WAKES

(MR. AND MRS. ABEL ARE APPROACHING A STRANGE PAPUAN VILLAGE)

In that village they found all the men standing in array against them, armed with spears and bows and arrows, with hate in their eyes. All the women and children had been sent out of the village.

When the women and children are sent out of the village in that way, it means death.

" What can we do ? " asked Mrs. Abel of her husband.

" We can do nothing but hope," he answered. " Let us sit down on that fallen tree."

So they sat down together on the trunk of the tree, looking death in the face.

But Mrs. Abel, glancing to the left, saw in the doorway of a hut a Papuan woman lying. God had given to her also the most beautiful present in the world—a baby girl. She was only a few hours old, and the mother was too ill to be moved from the village with the other women and children.

Mrs. Abel, forgetting all about the savages with their spears and bows and arrows and the death that faced her, and only remembering the little girl she herself had lost, jumped up and ran towards the hut, picked up the little brown baby, and hugged her up to herself with mother-love, kissed her and gave her back to the Papuan mother. Every man in the village threw down his spear, threw down his bow and arrows. They asked the missionaries what they could give them. . . . Deep down in those men, under their horrible cruelty, was a sleeping beauty.

BASIL MATHEWS.

61. A PACIFIST NATION

The independent State of Luxemburg with an area of 999 square miles and a population of 300,000 is wedged in between France, Germany and Belgium.

Although entitled under the Treaty of Versailles to re-arm and re-build her forts, Luxemburg chooses to remain undefended without soldiers and without arms.

The Luxemburger Wort, the leading newspaper, in its issue of June 14th, 1935, gives the following as the reasons :

" To arm and join in a military alliance would mean sacrificing our independence. It would make enemies for us among other nations. Armed France feels no more secure than unarmed Luxemburg.

If we are invaded our chances of good treatment are better if we have incurred no nation's suspicion by arms and alliances.

Should Divine providence one day—let us hope that it will not be in the near future—want us to perish with the other nations in the universal fury of a new slaughter, then let us die free and innocent, keeping in our hands the sparkling weapon of our right, of our independence, our freedom and our neutrality, not as cowards who wanted to find a safety which nobody can give, and who have sold their most beautiful good, their independence."

62. IN THE HANDS OF PIRATES

A MISSIONARY IN CHINA

The following letter, written on the high seas from a ship in the hands of Chinese pirates, has been received in London from Miss Monsen, the elderly Norwegian missionary whose capture on board the Chinese steamer Peiching was reported in " The Times" of April 29th, 1929.

OFF THE COAST OF SHANTUNG

April 25.—On the morning of April 19 I left the China Inland Mission at Tientsin to go to Hwang-hsien by steamer. One of the men on the ship consented to give me his cabin on board, at twice the price he had paid for it. This man proved a real friend to me when he found that his cabin was not looted because I was in it. The crossing should take 15 to 17 hours and I was going to rough it for a night without bedding ; but I stayed 28 days on that ship. Unknown to us we had robbers on board. Right from Tientsin, on the way down the river, I had been giving them tracts, believing those I saw in the second class to be ordinary business men.

Just before daybreak there was an awful yell, and the cabin doors were roughly opened by men with pistols in their hands, and I heard shots on all sides. All the passengers were commanded to leave their cabins and everything they had there at once. I just remained where I was.

The steamer was stopped on the high seas. The first robber that entered my cabin said " We are Governor Djang's soldiers, and have come to take care of the ship." I could not help laughing aloud. " So I hear," I answered. When he had got all the information he wanted he left, saying, " Don't be afraid." " Do I look it ? " I asked. " No," he admitted. The next visitor pointed at my watch and said, " Hide that somewhere, or it will be taken," and left. I took the hint, little dreaming that the same man would come for it when he got a better opportunity. Then came a boy. He said he was eighteen, and pointed his pistol at me saying, "Have you got a watch?" "Yes." "Make a present of it to me and I will be your friend." "I don't usually make friends in that way, nor do I need such friends. I am not used to giving such presents to people I do not know. Did your parents teach you to ask such presents of people?" He winced and again pointed his pistol at me, while I quietly repeated "No. You cannot possibly shoot me without special permission from God." How often that sentence was repeated that day! Another man came and sent the boy off. The Lord protected my cabin door. I wish I had counted the many, many times those men were going to enter my cabin and just passed by.

GREEDY HANDS

The man who had asked me to hide my watch came again and asked for it. He examined it closely and offered me money for it. I refused to sell, and he took it. Half an hour later came the first man that had entered my cabin, and this time I had a long talk with him. He said they could not make a proper living in the Army any longer, so had had to find another means of livelihood. He asked if they had taken anything from me. "Yes, my watch." "Who took it? I will bring it back to you." It really was a surprise that he did so. Before leaving again he whispered, "Don't leave this cabin while we are on board, if you want to keep it and your other things. Tell anyone that comes along that the General does not want you to be disturbed." My things were left alone from that time, though many greedy eyes and fingers went over them again and again those 23 days they were on board.

For a day and a night the ship did not move. On the second day a boat with a supply of ammunition came up with the ship. The ammunition was stored in the next cabin to mine.

During the next five or six days, junks after junks were looted, and the ship filled with loot. At different places junks came out from the shore to fetch the loot. All the fare on board was loot. I objected to eating loot, and told them plainly why. I happened to have an unusual supply of biscuits, apples, and chocolate, which, very economically used, lasted me 10 days. The General's room was next to mine, and I heard many a heated debate through the thin walls. Constantly I heard them debating about carrying me off with them. Once I heard a voice asking very impatiently why they could not loot me like the other passengers. "Leave her alone," said the General.

May 3.—I am still here, hidden behind my raincoat hung across the door. We have not moved since I last wrote. No one knows where the ship is. I understand they are demanding $200,000 from the steamship company in ransom. Again and again I have been able to speak to these men heart to heart, even to the General. Thank God I have been kept entirely from fear all the time, even from impatience after freedom. I am a big puzzle to the pirates. The 200 passengers look worn and yellow, full of fear, as they are stuffed together down below.

DELIVERANCE

May 11.—The last four days there has been an intense struggle going on between the powers of darkness and light. Somebody must be on the ship's track; the robbers' spies are coming and going all the time. The pirates—there were 20 to begin with and as many as 50 or 60 at times—are ready to leave the ship at a moment's notice. They are on the watch all the time, and 40 or 50 junks keep alongside the ship. They have been on the point of leaving the ship several times, taking me with them. At the last moment something would stop them. Once a sudden hurricane drove the junks from the ship's side. Another time I heard a man ordered to come and tell me to get ready to go into the boat with them. He opened my door and we stood looking at each other, but not one word was he allowed to say. He shut my door with a bang and said : " I cannot say that to her ; she is good, and it would be wronging her a second time."

May 13.—Yesterday deliverance came. In two hours they were all gone. They suddenly saw something which made them go. All the ammunition was divided between them, and we heard the sound of a warship's gun.

We had a race for two hours with the warship. By five in the afternoon the last robber had left the ship. About 20 passengers were carried off but left behind by the robbers in the junks when they ran for their lives. Up to the last the question of carrying me off was a problem to them. They needed a foreign face to protect them, so they said. In the end my refusal to eat of their loot was my salvation. A voice said, " No, she would only hinder us. She has not been eating anything for more than 20 days."

It was lovely to see the joy of the passengers that night. " We have had a sword through our hearts for 23 days, but now it has been taken out." They had all been wanting to talk to me but had not dared. Some of them went over next morning to have wireless messages sent off from the warship, and heard there that the warship had been in search of us for a fortnight or more, unable to find any trace of us. Our hiding-place was a master stroke of the robbers.

"*The Times*," June 29, 1929.

63. A NEGRO PRACTISES DIRECT ACTION

The other day one of the young secretaries in the American F.o.R., a coloured boy, was on a speaking trip in the South and broke over the middle wall of race segregation which is customary in certain States, by sitting on a seat in an autobus in a section reserved for whites. The bus driver telephoned ahead to the police, so that just outside of a city where the bus was going four police ruffians halted the bus and, entering, demanded in insulting language that young Bayard Rustin get out of the seat he was occupying. The rest of the story is best told in his own words by his letter. After describing how the policemen threw him to the floor, beat and kicked him and dragged him outside, he wrote :

I jumped to my feet, held out my arms parallel to the ground and said, " There is not need to beat me. I am not resisting you." At this point, three white men, obviously Southerners from their speech, came out of the bus. They said, " Why do that to him ? He has done nothing. Why not treat him like a human being ? He is not resisting you." One little fellow grabbed the policeman's club as he was about to strike me, saying, " Don't you do that ! " The police was about to strike him when I said to him, " Please don't do that. There is no need, for I am protected well. There is no need to fight. I thank you just the same."

The three white friends began to collect my clothes and luggage, which the bus driver had thrown out of the bus to the side of the road. One elderly man asked the police where they were taking me. They said " Nashville ". He promised me that he would be there to see that I got justice.

During the thirteen-mile hectic ride to town, they continuously called me every kind of name and said anything which might incite me to violence. I sat absolutely still, looking them straight in the eye whenever they dared to face me. The fact that they could not look at me gave me courage and hope, for I knew that they were aware of injustice. This made them quite open for development.

When I reached Nashville, they went through my luggage and papers. They were most interested in the *Christian Century* and *Fellowship*.

Finally, the captain said, " Come here, Nigger."

I walked directly to him.

" What can I do for you ? " I said.

" Nigger," he said, " you're supposed to be scared when you come in here."

" I am fortified by truth, justice and Christ," I said, " there is no need for me to fear."

He was flabbergasted. For a time he said nothing. Then he walked to another officer and said, in his frustration, " I believe the Nigger's crazy."

I waited there an hour and a half. The next thing I knew I was taken for a long ride across town. At the courthouse I was taken into the office of the Assistant District Attorney. As I entered the door I heard someone say, " Say, you coloured fellow, hey ! " I looked round and there was the white gentleman who said he would see that I got justice.

The District Attorney questioned me about my life, the *Christian Century*, the F.o.R., pacifism and the war for one half hour. He then asked the police to tell their side of the story. They told several lies. He then asked me to tell my side. This I did, calling upon the policemen to substantiate me at each point. The District Attorney dismissed me. I waited an hour longer in a dark room all alone. Then he came in and said very kindly, " You may go, *Mr.* Rustin."

In amazement I left the courthouse, being all the stronger a believer in the non-violent approach, for I am certain that I was called *Mr.*, that I was assisted by the elderly gentleman, and assisted by the three men in the bus, because I had, without fear, faced four policemen, saying, " There is no need to beat me. I offer you no resistance."

The following account of a similar triumph for courageous non-violence is given by the same friend :

Between speaking engagements in a Midwestern college town I went into a small restaurant to buy a hamburger and a glass of milk. I had not been sitting in the restaurant long before I noticed that I was being systematically ignored. After waiting about ten minutes I decided that the conflict had to be faced. I moved to one corner, stood directly before a waitress so that she could not overlook me, and said, " I would like to have a hamburger." " I'm sorry," she replied, " but we can't serve . . . er, er . . . you, er . . . coloured people here." " Who's responsible for this ? " I asked. She made her reply in two gestures—the first indicating a rather buxom woman standing in the rear ; and the second, a finger to the lip, an obvious appeal for me not to involve her in any way.

I walked directly to the woman standing near the coffee urn in the rear of the restaurant. " I would like to know why it is impossible for me to be served here ? " I asked. " Well . . . well, er . . . " she stuttered, " it's . . . er . . . it's because we don't do that in this town. They don't serve coloured people in any of the restaurants." " Why ? " I asked. " It's because they're dirty," she said, " and they won't work, and because if I served them everybody would walk out, and then what would happen to my business ? "

I took from my pocket a report compiled by the local F.o.R. Together we thought through many of the facts which explained the juvenile delinquency, unemployment, boisterousness, and other conditions and qualities allegedly peculiar to Negroes. One by one we eliminated all of the problems which would interfere with my being served, except the economic one.

" Have you ever served Negroes ? " I asked. " No," she replied warily. " Then why do you believe that doing so would offend your customers ? " I then appealed to her to make an experiment in the extension of democracy. After some hesitation she agreed to the following terms : that I would sit conspicuously in the front of the restaurant for ten minutes, during which time I would not eat my hamburger, and we would count the number of people who left on my account or who, being about to enter, retreated. If we saw one such person I would leave myself. Or if we did not I was to be served.

I waited fifteen minutes. Then she approached me, picked up the cold hamburger, placed a hot one before me, and said simply, " What will you have to drink with it ? "

I have been given to understand by Negroes and whites in the local situation that Mrs. Duffy continues to serve Negroes without embarrassment or conflict, which is indeed a courageous thing in the circumstances.

From the International Fellowship of Reconciliation.

I cannot think that all people are bad, even the worst of the Christians, for to-day I had an experience—just an hour ago—that makes me think that outside of office and business, outside of riches and honours, there are small happenings which touch a man's heart, and make him feel that humanity is not all iron and gain and falsehood.

For to-day this yamen which for twenty-four years had been mine, was the destination of a great mission, such as never came within the compound before. I nearly wept to receive them.

Two native Christians came all the way from that miserable town in Japan to bring me here medicines for my head, and to see if I was getting better! I wonder if this is because Christianity teaches such things? It must be, for the Japanese are a race that assume to be strong in matters of physical pain, and they are a people that hate the outsider—the Chinese most of all. Therefore, it must be some new idea that this man and boy got into their heads to make them do such a thing.

With my own eyes I saw them coming up the steps of the yamen, and at first I told Len to send them away—as if I were the proprietor of the place; but I soon saw that they were Japanese, and wondered what they might want of me, or if it was me they desired to see. Len let them in, but for a long time we could not learn just what was desired; for the man spoke his own tongue, or a dialect of it, and I could gather but a few words.

Ling-ho, one of my interpreters, being sent for, I was amazed to learn that the strange man was one of a number of native converts who had called to see me in my sick room, when I was recovering from the effects of the madman's bullet in my skull and as I looked at him I saw that he was telling the truth for I recognised him. His name, he said, was Sato, and the boy that accompanied him was his thirteen-year-old son.

Sato said that all the native Christians in the little mission of Ketuki, near Moji—the mission that had at first sent the delegation to my sick room with flowers—had talked about me every day since I was there, and had prayed to the Christian God for my recovery. He said that they, his mission friends, did not believe in war or killing, and that they had understood that I had come to put a stop to the war.

" Were we not right, your Excellency? " he asked.

" Yes, Mr. Sato," I said, " you were right. I went to try and stop the war. There has not been any since, has there? "

He answered, No, and said I was a great and good man. Then he explained that all his friends were very anxious to know how I was getting along. Sometimes, he said, they would hear that I was entirely well, and again it would be reported that I was dead; so they couldn't stand the uncertainty any longer, and collected money between them and sent Sato with a message of goodwill and some herb medicines.

I took the medicines and had my two visitors served with the nicest kind of boiled chicken, some chicken and tongue on crackers, rice, cakes and tea. I wanted them to stay with me for a few days, telling them that I would treat them well; but Mr. Sato said that he was already sick unto death to get back home, and that he had once or twice nearly turned back, especially as his son was so lonely. Besides, he said, he had been driven almost to distraction, not knowing whether he would find me here, at Peking, or in the South.

When they were ready to go, I gave them a big bundle of presents of all kinds for their friends at Ketuki, 200 taels for the mission, and as much more to reimburse them for the outlay of the journey. This last he did not want to accept, saying that, as he had funds sufficient to take him home, he was fearful that the friends who had sent him might not like it. But I prevailed upon him to take the money.

I think this Christianity makes poor and lowly people bold and unafraid, for before Sato and his boy left he wanted to know if they might pray for me. I said they could, expecting that he meant when they got back home again; but he said something to the little son, and they knelt right there at the door and said a prayer. I could not keep my heart from thumping in my bosom as I watched that poor man and his frightened little boy praying to God—the God that will deal with me and with them and all mankind—that I might be well of my injuries.

I was sorry to see them go.

In this old yamen, which for twenty odd years was mine, strange scenes have been enacted, great councils held, and midnight conferences affecting the whole world have taken place. I have received royalties and dukes, ambassadors, ministers, murderers, robbers and beggars. Men have been sentenced to death from here, others have been made glad with leases of lands, railroad contracts, or the gift of public office. But during each and every occurrence, whatever its nature, I have been complete master of my house and myself—until an hour ago. Then it was that for the first time did I believe the favour was being conferred on me. (Li was not master of the yamen when he wrote this, but was simply making it his headquarters during his stay in Tientsin.)

Poor, good Mr. Sato, all the way from Japan to offer a Christian prayer for the " heathen " old Viceroy ! I did not know that anyone outside my own family cared enough about me for such a thing.

I do not love the Japanese, but perhaps Christianity would help them !

From *Memoirs of the Viceroy Li Hung Chang.*
(Constable), London, 1913

65. LEONARD FELL AND THE HIGH-WAYMAN

Leonard Fell, when travelling alone, was attacked by a high-wayman, who demanded his money, which he gave him ; then he desired to have his horse ; Leonard dismounted and let him take it. Then feeling the power of truth rise in his mind, he turned to the robber, and under its authority solemnly warned him of the evil of his ways ; but he, flying into a passion, asked the Friend why he preached to him, and threatened to blow out his brains. But Leonard replying to this effect, " Though I would not give my life for my money or my horse, I would give it to save thy soul," so struck the astonished robber that he declared, if he was such a man as that he would take neither his money nor his horse from him ; and, returning both to the faithful Friend, went his way, leaving Leonard to the enjoyment of that peace attending the honest discharge of his conscience, to obtain which he had not counted his life dear.

From *The Journal of George Fox.*

66. MEXICO'S NEW PRESIDENT, 1941

Avila Camacho—he uses both his family names, Avila his father's and Camacho his mother's—is himself 43. Reared by well-to-do parents on a ranch and schooled as an accountant, he joined the Mexican Revolution at 17. Mexicans cannot deeply love a politician who was not a soldier in some revolution. He rose swiftly through the ranks and became a brigadier general at 27. But he was a very special kind of soldier—so special that his political opponents later nicknamed him El Soldado Des-conocido, the unknown soldier. His speciality was persuasion.

Instead of meeting rebellious generals in frontal conflict, he would take an airplane, fly to their camp, sit them down on a log and pacify them with sympathetic conversation and promises —which, surprisingly enough, he kept. The rebels he subdued by oratory often became his greatest admirers.

From *The Reader's Digest*, February 1941.

67. TEN THOUSAND FRIENDS

In ancient times, Kwen,[1] the father of Yu, built a city wall twenty-four feet in height, in consequence of which all the feudal princes abandoned their allegiance, and dwellers beyond the sea became false and crafty. Yu[2] knew that the Empire was infected with disloyalty, so he pulled down the wall and filled up the city moat, distributed largess among the people, and burnt all the armour and muniments of war. Thus by a display of kindness he caused those who dwelt beyond the sea to come and willingly offer their allegiance, and people from all sides to bring tribute ; and when the feudal princes assembled at T'u-shan, bearing their jade insignia, they represented no less than ten thousand states.

From *The History of Great Light*.

68. THE CANADIAN SOLDIER WHO COULD NOT KILL

A Canadian soldier when on leave from the war became influenced by Quaker ideas as to the divine soul in every man which it is wrong for a fellow-man to take away. He returned to his Unit and explained to his Commanding Officer that he could not kill any more. The officer liked him because he was a good soldier and said he should hate to have him shot. The young man suggested that the King's Regulations are precise—You're shot (1) for showing cowardice in face of the enemy ; (2) for throwing away arms in a similar case. He agreed he would do neither. So he joined his fellow-soldiers going over the top regularly but with his rifle across his arm. His officer permitted this, his N.C.O.

[1] Kwen was Minister of Works for the Emperor Yao in 2297 B.C.
[2] Yu the Great rendered faithful services to the Emperors Yao and Shun. On the death of Shun in 2208 B.C., after observing a three years' period of mourning, in 2205 B.C. Yu succeeded him, becoming the founder of the Dynasty of Hia.

was furious, sending the young man out on every raid. Once only three of the raiders came back of a whole Company and once the young soldier had over 20 bullet holes in his clothes but only a scratch. Finally he found himself left in a trench alone and along it comes a German " mopping up " with his bayonet " at ready ". The soldier put his own rifle against the trench bank and went towards the German. Knowing only two German words he put out his hands to shake hands remarking " Man " and " Liebe ". The German stopped, laughed, took his hand. They sat down together in silence, then shook hands again and parted. So his life at the front went on. The officer gave him his sergeant's stripes, perhaps to rid him of the pestering of the other N.C.O. When the story was told the man was occupied in un-military duties in California, presumably having been allowed to leave the army.

69. ONE ENGLISHMAN'S WAY IN INDIA

At least one Englishman attacked by an Indian mob has met their violence with non-violence.

He is Mr. Lewis, former assistant editor of the " Statist ", of London, who is now engaged in buying supplies for China.

He was travelling near Benares when a crowd of 200 attacked him, smashed the windows of the train compartment in which he was the only passenger, and hurled stones and broken glass at him, gashing his forehead.

Then the mob crowded his carriage and hit him with lathis, Mr. Lewis sat with folded arms and offered no resistance.

This nonplussed the attackers, who asked him if he was a Hindu —a sign they were uncomfortable and prepared to accept any excuse to call off the attack.

At that moment Mr. Lewis's Indian servants arrived and blandly explained that he was not only Hindu but Chinese as well.

ASH FOR ANTISEPTIC

Profuse apologies and long speeches on both sides ensued, while, in the absence of iodine, the Indians smoked cigarettes hard to provide ash which, they insisted, was a first-class antiseptic to smear over Mr. Lewis's gashed forehead.

As the train was about to leave a boy wriggled through the crowd yelling, " I want to smash the lavatory ".

The mob leader turned courteously to Mr. Lewis and asked, "May the child smash the lavatory?"

Mr. Lewis replied that according to his principles of non-violence he could not approve so violent an action, but likewise he was unable physically to oppose the child.

The small boy smashed the lavatory.

From *The News Chronicle*, August 29, 1942.

70. THE STORY OF WATERFORD BRIDGE

About 1861, in the days of the Fenian agitators in Ireland, an attempt at open rebellion was made near Carrick-on-Suir. Hundreds of young men left their homes and offices to join it, but to their dismay a fierce snowstorm came on and daunted the ardour of the ill-fed, ill-clad "army". The bridge over the river Suir at Waterford was a large wooden one, known as the "bundle of sticks," the private property of some of the leading Quaker families, held under an old charter. It was known that the rebels must return to Waterford by it, so the military took possession of it. But the Waterford Quakers told them not to trespass on their private property, and when the soldiers explained why they had done it the Quakers replied, "Shure, we know all about that; you just run along home, and we'll look after the rebels." When the latter came along, cold and crestfallen, the Friends only let them pass one or two at a time, and the young men hid amongst the merchandise on the quay, afraid to be seen. The Quakers persuaded them to come out, and escorted them back to their employers who, in most cases, agreed to take them back, and forgive their misbehaviour. A much happier ending than shooting them on the bridge.

ERNEST H. BENNIS.

71. A CHILDREN'S ARMY

During a protest strike in Aarhus, in 1944, according to the Swedish newspaper *Aftontidningen*, a crowd of children paraded through the streets and attracted other children as they marched along. Finally, there were in all about 1,000 children from two to fifteen years' old, surging forward, pulling down German road signs, indications of the occupation of their country, Denmark.

The Danish police and the Germans were said to have been helpless against this demonstration of unarmed children.

Worldover Press.

72. THE NEGRO SINGER AND THE POLICEMEN

Roland Hayes, the famous Negro singer, tells how he was set upon late one night by four policemen who manhandled him without the least provocation. Their attitude was brutal, bordering on the sadistic, and they gave full expression to their hatred, not for him alone, but for his race. He was one lone and defenceless Negro, at the mercy of four white men, unrepresentative of, and a disgrace to, the white race.

" Did you get angry and fight them back ? " I asked. " How could I ? " he replied, " I was no match physically for even one of them. But I *was* a match for them in another way, and so was able to overcome them. I brought to bear a power that no evil can stand against."

" What did you do ? " I asked, with intense interest. " I retired into God-consciousness," he replied. " I just prayed for the spirit of Christ to flow through me into the hearts of those misguided men. As I thus exercised spiritual thought-power, suddenly I had a feeling of being lifted high above this hatred, and I looked down upon them in compassion and pity. One policeman raised his pistol with the intent of hitting me with its butt. While his arm was raised a curious and bewildered expression came over his face. Slowly his poised arm dropped. He had been stopped by the tremendous power of the spirit, by God-consciousness."

Reprinted from " A Guide to Confident Living," published by The World's Work (1913) Ltd., Kingswood, Surrey.

73. THE INVASION OF CALIFORNIA

In 1875 a fleet of Chinese war junks set out to attack California. News had reached the Emperor in Peking that thousands of Chinese who had gone to California to work on the new raidroads were being cruelly mistreated and the enraged Emperor resolved to teach the United States a lesson that it would not soon forget. Eastward bound for Monterey sailed seven junks armed with brass cannon. The Emperor, however, not realising the size of the Pacific, had not sufficiently provisioned the fleet, and before the voyage was half over the sailors faced death from thirst. Just in time a rainstorm came ; quickly the sails were lowered and used as troughs to catch the rain. At last the doughty fleet reached Monterey ; fifty gunners stood by the cannon ready to blast the city to pieces if it put up a fight. But far from resisting, the people of Monterey were so delighted with this unexpected visit of Chinese war junks, that the whole town came down to the shore to welcome the invaders. The pigtailed warriors, overwhelmed with hospitality, liked California so much that they refused to go home. The older men got jobs on the railroads, and the younger ones stayed on in Monterey as fishermen.

The Story of His Life's Adventures.
RICHARD HALLIBURTON.

74. DANCING WITH THE PARTISANS IN RUSSIA

A railwayman named Lilje was sent to Russia in 1943 during the German occupation, to take charge of a station near Smolensk. His predecessor had been a harsh man, who treated the Russians under him in an unfair way. The consequence was that several times already he had heard the bullets of Partisans whistling near his head when he ventured to go out of his office in the dark, as the region was infested with Partisans.

But Lilje said to his Russian workers : " I shall give you a certain amount of work every day, and when you have finished it, you may go home." At first they did not believe him, but soon they found that he kept his word, and friendly relations were established between them.

One day, an old Russian peasant invited Lilje to go with him to a wedding party in a remote village. Upon arrival at the village, the old man said to Lilje, who was wearing German uniform : " Now, for your own safety, and that of all of us, it would be better for you to give that pistol and dagger of yours to me, and I shall lock them up till to-morrow, and while you are dancing you will not need them. Lilje, after some hesitation agreed. Then the celebration started, and Lilje had a glorious time, dancing all night with the young people of the neighbourhood.

Next morning, the old peasant handed his arms back to him, and drove him back to his station. On the way, he said : " I will tell you why I thought it better you should not have your weapons. All those young men who were dancing in the same room with you are fierce Partisans, who have sworn to kill any German soldier they can get hold of. Amongst them, you were safer unarmed."

"But," replied Lilje, I *am* a German soldier! Why did they not kill me, as they have sworn to?"

"Oh! no", said the old man, "you are not a German soldier, you are a reasonable man, who is kind to the Russian workers. That is known all over the country here, and nobody has anything against a man like you."

Story told by Lilje to Heinz Kraschutzki.

75. THE POWER OF MUSIC AND KINDNESS

When the Russians conquered Berlin, street by street, I was still far away, in a Spanish prison. In our little house, there were my wife, our 20 year old daughter and three old ladies of about 70.

The Russians had been through a very hard time, so when suddenly the Armistice came, and the steady danger was over, their desire naturally was for relaxation, which, of course, meant danger for young girls, though the Russian Commander did his best to protect them.

My wife knew that the Russians are very fond of music, so when groups of Russian soldiers banged at the door, she would open it, and let them in, smiling, to the drawing-room, asking them whether they would like to hear some music. Certainly they would! So they sat down, and she played, leaving the rest to Beethoven, Bach and Mozart. They listened with rapt attention, sometimes for hours, and, when leaving, thanked her for her kindness.

She was naturally anxious for her daughter. One day, a Russian soldier seized the girl by the wrist. My wife tried to interfere, but was thrown aside. Then one of the old ladies, who was very small, intervened She put her hand on the soldier's shoulder, and began to caress his cheek, saying: "You are not a bad fellow. I know you are not! You will not do any harm to this girl, will you?" The Russian probably did not understand her words, but he let the girl free, and went away, in some confusion.

One of the Russians advised my wife that it was not safe for so pretty a girl to stay in the house at night. They should go to a neighbour's house, where there were 15 or 20 Germans, and then she would be safe. My wife followed his advice, and all was well.

In fact, nobody in my house was hurt. But a rich man nearby, when asked if he had wine in the house, protested there was none. The Russians said they would shoot him if there was, and finding it downstairs did as they said, and he lost his life for his wine.

Heinz Kraschutzki.

76. BRAVE WORDS WIN RESPECT

Mrs. H.—is a German woman living in a western suburb of Berlin. She is known for her impetuous temperament and unruly tongue.

She did all she could to help poor Jews when persecuted, hiding them as best she could. She was at the Town Hall one day towards the end of the war, when some of the Gestapo warned her and some other people not to say a word against the régime. But Mrs. H.— lost her temper " And I will talk ! " she yelled. " It is a shame what is being done. I don't hate the Jews, no, I don't. And I don't love your Hitler, who is responsible for all this misery." Then she left the room, but the police brought her back, wanting to carry her away, but some neighbours intervened. " Remember," they said, " that all these women have had to spend six nights in their cellars while the bombs were dropping. They are nervous, and Mrs. H.— hardly knows what she says when she loses her temper ". So they let her go.

Some months later, the Russians were there, and soon Mrs. H.— was in trouble again. She was accused, to the local Russian Commander of having insulted Russian soldiers.

" Is it true," he asked sternly, " that you have said that Russian soldiers are stealing watches ? "

" Certainly, it is true."

" Why do you say such things ? "

" Because they took my watch from my wrist. Isn't it a shame."

" Now listen," thundered the Russian Officer, " did you protest in the same vigorous way, when the Nazis ill-treated the Jews ? "

" Certainly I did."

Someone then told the Officer that Mrs. H.— had, in fact, tried to help persecuted Jews, and had been very impertinent to the Gestapo also.

At this, the Russian Officer answered :—

" When you say that a Russian soldier took your watch from your wrist, I think I must believe it. When I am told that you are a woman who protested against the cruelties of the Nazis, then I respect you. I always hold in high esteem people who speak the truth and have courage. You go home now, and nothing will happen to you. And try to forget all the wrongs you have suffered."